TAKING

Social Emotional Learning

Schoolwide

Other ASCD publications by the author:

The Formative Five: Fostering Grit, Empathy, and Other Success Skills Every Student Needs

Fostering Grit: How do I prepare my students for the real world? (ASCD Arias)

The Art of School Leadership

Becoming a Multiple Intelligences School

ASCD MEMBER BOOK

Many ASCD members received this book as a member benefit upon its initial release.

Learn more at **www.ascd.org/memberbooks**

Thomas R. Hoerr

TAKING ●●●●●

Social Emotional Learning

Schoolwide

The Formative Five Success
Skills for Students and Staff

Alexandria, VA USA

1703 N. Beauregard St. • Alexandria, VA 22311-1714 USA
Phone: 800-933-2723 or 703-578-9600 • Fax: 703-575-5400
Website: www.ascd.org • E-mail: member@ascd.org
Author guidelines: www.ascd.org/write

Ronn Nozoe, *Interim CEO and Executive Director*; Stefani Roth, *Publisher*; Genny Ostertag, *Director, Content Acquisitions*; Julie Houtz, *Director, Book Editing & Production*; Liz Wegner, *Editor*; Judi Connelly, *Senior Art Director*; Mary Duran, *Graphic Designer*; Masie Chong, *Graphic Designer*; Keith Demmons, *Senior Production Designer*; Kelly Marshall, *Interim Manager, Production Services*; Trinay Blake, *E-Publishing Specialist*

PAPERBACK ISBN: 978-1-4166-2837-8   ASCD product #120014
PDF E-BOOK ISBN: 978-1-4166-2839-2; see Books in Print for other formats.
Quantity discounts are available: e-mail programteam@ascd.org or call 800-933-2723, ext. 5773, or 703-575-5773. For desk copies, go to www.ascd.org/deskcopy.

ASCD Member Book No. FY20-3 (Dec. 2019 P). ASCD Member Books mail to Premium (P), Select (S), and Institutional Plus (I+) members on this schedule: Jan, PSI+; Feb, P; Apr, PSI+; May, P; Jul, PSI+; Aug, P; Sep, PSI+; Nov, PSI+; Dec, P. For current details on membership, see www.ascd.org/membership.

Library of Congress Cataloging-in-Publication Data
Names: Hoerr, Thomas R., 1945- author.
Title: Taking social-emotional learning schoolwide : the formative five
    success skills for students and staff / Thomas R. Hoerr.
Description: Alexandria, VA : ASCD, [2020] | Includes bibliographical
    references and index.
Identifiers: LCCN 2019033044 (print) | LCCN 2019033045 (ebook) | ISBN
    9781416628378 (paperback) | ISBN 9781416628392 (pdf)
Subjects: LCSH: Affective education. | Social learning. | School
    environment--Social aspects. | Emotional intelligence.
Classification: LCC LB1072 .H64 2020 (print) | LCC LB1072 (ebook) | DDC
    370.15/34--dc23
LC record available at https://lccn.loc.gov/2019033044
LC ebook record available at https://lccn.loc.gov/2019033045

29 28 27 26 25 24 23 22 21 20   1 2 3 4 5 6 7 8 9 10 11 12

TAKING ●●●●● Social Emotional Learning
Schoolwide

Preface

Who you are is more important than what you know.

Important as they are, academics should be the floor of our expectations for our students' growth, not the ceiling. We need to intentionally teach children social-emotional learning and the Formative Five success skills of *empathy, self-control, integrity, embracing diversity,* and *grit* so they can succeed in life. In this book, I address each of the Formative Five success skills through the lens of John Coleman's "six components of a great culture" (2013): *vision/mission, values, practices, people, narrative,* and *place*. Of course, in the real world, distinctions among components of culture are not crystal clear; *people* engage in *practices* in various *places*, and a *narrative* emerges. This same overlap also applies to the Formative Five skills: *empathy* and *embracing diversity* are closely related, for example, as are *self-control* and *grit*. Seeking and recognizing opportunities for synergy among both the Formative Five skills and Coleman's six components will vastly increase the likelihood of success. While this book flows from my previous book, *The Formative Five*, it can be read on its own (although, of course, I heartily recommend reading *The Formative Five*!).

John Coleman wisely notes that for our values to matter, they must be embedded in what we do, part of our everyday routines and actions. This is undoubtedly true: Our habits carry us through the day without requiring much contemplation or decision making on our part. Chances are that you don't recall much of your travel to work this morning, for example—it just happened.

In *The Power of Habit* (2012), Charles Duhigg says,

Most of the choices we make each day may feel like the products of well-considered decision making, but they're not. They're habits. And though each habit means relatively little on its own, over time, the meals we order, what we say to our kids each night, whether we save or spend, how often we exercise, and the way we organize our thoughts and work routine have enormous impacts on our health, productivity, financial security, and happiness. (pp. xv–xvi)

Of course, the habits Duhigg describes create our culture, so it is really culture that we take for granted. This is especially the case in settings like organizations, where we work with others toward a common goal. Our habits save time, energy, and thought—sometimes. Other times, our habits aren't productive. Perhaps the situation has changed, but our habits haven't; possibly a habit isn't as effective as we think, but we don't get the feedback to step back and question it; maybe we've developed a habit to insulate us against coworkers rather than work with them. In any of these cases (and in many more), the habit doesn't help us serve our students or ourselves. We need to examine and reflect on all our habits, even the good ones—in fact, how do we know whether a habit is good if we don't?

As Duhigg notes, "People [can't] detect most of the bad smells in their lives. If you live with nine cats, you become desensitized to their scent. If you smoke cigarettes, it damages your olfactory capacities so much that you can't smell smoke anymore" (p. 43). On a less malodorous note, here's a personal example: For years, I was known for my outrageous ties in school (and by outrageous, I mean ugly). Kids and faculty members delighted in making comments, faces, and sarcastic remarks about them. But I wore these kinds of ties so often that I became accustomed to the conflagrations of colors and clashing patterns. My habit, in other words, had inured me to the visual pain that my ties caused others.

The good news is that we don't have to be shackled by our habits. We can choose the habits that we want and consciously work to develop them, and by doing so transparently—acknowledging the focus and including others in our efforts—we increase the likelihood of success. We can also work to rid ourselves of habits that are harmful. (Yes, I am working on selecting more attractive ties—or at least considering whether they clash with my shirts.)

This is an exciting time to be an educator because we know more about how children learn than we ever have before and we understand the role we can play in shaping their futures. We must recognize and support the whole child. Students are more than stanines. Let's learn together!

1

SEL: It's About Time!

- Teachers: It's a Tuesday at 10:00 a.m. Picture two students: the one who sits in the third row, second seat, and the one in the first row, third seat. Consider these two children's faces as you read this chapter.
- Administrators: Please think of the last two times you spoke to two or three students. Consider these children's faces as you read this chapter.

Perhaps Albert Einstein put it best when he said, "Not everything that can be counted counts, and not everything that counts can be counted." It's only natural to focus on qualities that can be readily measured, compared, and shared. Unfortunately, that approach leads us to focus on discrete topics that can be assessed by multiple-choice tests. As a beginning 5th grade teacher, I was aware of this obsession because my principal continually talked about the need to raise our school's test scores, and it was a topic at most faculty meetings. Our school was in a high-poverty area and we had myriad issues to address—school safety was a concern, we had several new teachers, student discipline was a challenge, and so on—yet our strongest focus by far was on standardized tests.

1

This inordinate emphasis on the results from a few hours of tests administered during one week in the spring caused me to question the validity of the tests. I wondered what score would be generated if an answer sheet were submitted with random responses. What if the multiple-choice response bubbles on the answer sheet were filled in to create a nice, wavy pattern, irrespective of the questions that were asked? Would that yield terrible results, or might the randomness lead to an average score? Could pure luck lead to an above-average score? What an interesting question! (I am sure that you can see where this is heading.)

I decided to find out by completing and submitting a random-response sheet, naively thinking, "What could go wrong?" Not wanting to penalize any of my students by submitting this answer sheet with their name, I created a new student, Sam Suedo (my not-so-clever way of writing *pseudo*, hoping it wouldn't be noticed), and included Sam's answer sheet in my class' packet when I submitted it to the main office. So far, so good.

What I didn't realize was that before submitting the completed tests to be scored, the principal perused each teacher's class packet of answer sheets. I figured that something was amiss the next day when I found a note from the principal in my office mailbox, requesting that I see him *ASAP!* The combination of ASAP and an exclamation mark was not good, I knew. So much for "What could go wrong?"

The principal told me that he was surprised to see that an answer sheet from a new student was included in my class' packet. "Who is this Sam Suedo?" he asked, raising his voice and waving Sam's sheet in front of me. He was quite unhappy when I told him that I had created a fictitious student to see what standardized test score could be obtained from random responses. He exhaled loudly, rolled his eyes, and talked at length about how important it was for our school's students to do well on the test and how Mr. Suedo's scores would lower our school's average. I left his office a bit chagrined after Sam's unsubmitted answer sheet was torn into pieces and put in the waste can.

This fixation on test scores was driven home even further when I became a principal. In fact, during my final interview for the position, a one-to-one session with the superintendent, she told me that my priority would be to increase my school's test scores, period—that was the only educational issue we discussed. There was no mention of creativity, responsibility, or empathy. As principal, I attended the district's twice-monthly Board of Education meetings and regularly heard community members rail about our district's low test scores during the public forum at the beginning of the agenda. In fact, occasionally there were so many parents and community members wanting to complain or express concerns that the 10-minute open-microphone period was extended to an hour or longer. That made for a long night.

Many of the educators with whom I have talked and worked were bothered by this test-score orientation but were given neither the voice nor the opportunity to view students more broadly. The test-score mantra of legislators, school board members, the local press (schools' test scores were often front-page news), and some parents has made it very difficult to go beyond percentiles and address the needs of the whole child. That's because in most cases test scores have been viewed as *the* barometer of a school's quality. Educators share some of the responsibility for this because we typically haven't promoted any other formal, official data on student progress. If we only give parents one tool for measuring, why should we be surprised when that is the tool they use?

The lemming-like pursuit of high standardized scores received a significant boost from the 1983 report commissioned by President Ronald Reagan's education secretary, Terrel H. Bell, *A Nation at Risk: The Imperative for Educational Reform* (National Commission on Excellence in Education). It ominously noted, "If an unfriendly foreign power had attempted to impose on America the mediocre educational performance that exists today, we might well have viewed it as an act of war." Nearly 20 years later, in 2002, the federal government's No Child Left Behind (NCLB) legislation put even more emphasis on standardized tests. Educators' jobs were tied to students' test scores, as was the very continued existence of schools. (More than once I heard No Child Left Behind referred to as "No Teacher Left Standing.") In 2009, the Race to the Top program broadened the issues on which the government would focus but retained a strong emphasis on test scores.

In *The Tyranny of Metrics* (2018), Jerry Z. Muller says it well: "But what can be measured is not always worth measuring; what gets measured may have no relationship to what we really want to know" (p. 3). He goes on:

———————

> The unintended consequences of NCLB's testing-and-accountability regime are more tangible, and exemplify many of the characteristic pitfalls of metric fixation. Under NCLB, scores on standardized tests are the numerical metric by which success and failure are judged. And the stakes are high for teachers and principals, whose raises in salary and whose very jobs sometimes depend on this performance indicator. It is no wonder, then, that teachers (encouraged by their principals) divert class time toward the subjects tested—mathematics and English—and away from other subjects, such as history, social studies, art, music, and physical education. Instruction in math and English is narrowly focused on the sorts of skills required by the test, rather than broader cognitive processes: that is, students too often learn test-taking strategies rather than substantive knowledge. (p. 92)

Our battle for high test scores has caused us to lose the larger educational war. Children *do* need to learn to read, write, and calculate, but there is much more to consider in their education. We must also be focused on developing the kinds of people that these children will become. Will they be caring and productive, respectful and honest? Will they be good neighbors and understanding friends? Will they work to improve their communities? We need to prepare students to succeed in life, not just to do well in school, and for that we need to address their social-emotional learning (SEL).

Social-Emotional Learning (SEL)

The Robert Wood Johnson Foundation (n.d.) describes SEL as "a framework that focuses on the core social and emotional skills necessary for students of all ages to be healthy and successful." Evidence is clear that an educational SEL focus helps students in many ways. According to the foundation (2018), "There is strong scientific evidence that social and emotional learning (SEL) programs improve children's well-being, behavior, and academic outcomes. Evidence-based SEL programs at all levels from preschool to high school have been shown to promote the development of social, emotional, and academic competencies." The foundation also notes that a "cost-benefit analysis of six SEL programs found that for every dollar spent on SEL programming, society reaps an average benefit of $11 (2018)."

In their 2018 *Educational Leadership* article "SEL: What the Research Says," Joseph L. Mahoney and Roger P. Weissberg point to a meta-analysis of SEL programs that showed student participants had improved in SEL skills, attitudes toward self and others, positive social behavior, conduct problems, emotional distress, and academic performance. Further, they note that "SEL programs enhance academic achievement" (p. 34).

In another 2018 article for *Kappan Newsletter* titled "An Update on Social and Emotional Learning Outcome Research," Mahoney, Durlak, and Weissberg conclude from a meta-analysis of more than 300 research studies that "SEL programs appear to have as great a long-term impact on academic growth as has been found for programs designed specifically to support academic learning." They continue: "SEL programs are both feasible and effective in a variety of educational contexts around the world. SEL is neither a fad nor a flash in the pan but represents a useful way to improve students' social and emotional skills, which are associated with several positive behavioral and academic outcomes."

Momentum for using SEL to see the whole child is gaining. An article by John Fensterwald in *EdSource* (2019) notes:

A national survey this year of 15,000 teachers and 3,500 principals by the RAND Corporation found that 72 percent of principals said that promoting social and emotional skills was their top or one of their top priorities, with more principals in high-poverty schools rating it as their top priority. More than 80 percent of teachers said that social and emotional learning programs can improve school climate and student behavior; 64 percent said school achievement can be improved as well.

In this book, I expand the definition of SEL to also include adults. Although SEL efforts are directed at students, the adults in schools—teachers, administrators, support staff—will also need to be engaged in furthering their SEL. Kimberly A. Schonert-Reichl makes this point in her 2017 article for *The Future of Children* titled "Social and Emotional Learning and Teachers":

Teachers are the engine that drives social and emotional learning (SEL) programs and practices in schools and classrooms, and their own social-emotional competence and wellbeing strongly influence their students. Classrooms with warm teacher-child relationships support deep learning and positive social and emotional development among students. . . But when teachers poorly manage the social and emotional demands of teaching, students' academic achievement and behavior both suffer. If we don't accurately understand teachers' own social-emotional wellbeing and how teachers influence students' SEL . . . we can never fully know how to promote SEL in the classroom" (p. 137).

Simply put, we—the adults in schools, regardless of the professional roles we play or titles we hold—must also work on developing our SEL if we are to succeed in teaching these skills to our students. When we do this, everyone gains. (This topic is addressed more fully in Chapter 9, "Leadership Musings.")

What's in a Name?

One challenge administrators have faced in garnering support for SEL has been a lack of consensus on the terminology. *Noncognitive skills* is an oft-used term, but it isn't productive to define something by what it is not. (Further, I would argue that SEL has a strong cognitive component.) I've seen SEL skills referred to as *21st century skills; the second curriculum* has been used, too. Sometimes I see *soft skills*, which makes me cringe. At one point, the most common way to describe SEL skills was *emotional intelligence* (popularized by Daniel Goleman's 1995 book of the same name). Sometimes the teaching of SEL skills is referred to as *character education* or *social-emotional and character development*, but I do not see the need to refer to character as a component separate from SEL. Fortunately, consensus has emerged that *social-emotional learning*— coined by the Collaborative for Academic, Social, and Emotional Learning (CASEL) in 1994 (Gresham, 2018)—is the best term to describe this key area of human growth. And often using or saying the letters *SEL* suffices.

Figure 1.1 shows how CASEL's components of SEL align to the Formative Five success skills of empathy, self-control, integrity, embracing diversity, and grit. (See Figure 1.2 for a list of similar SEL components from a variety of organizations.) It's clear that each of the Formative Five skills has a unique identity, yet it's also clear, particularly as we think about implementation, that they often overlap. For example, there is a strong relationship between empathy and embracing diversity, which feed off one another: As our empathy increases, it becomes easier for us to embrace others who are different from us, and as we embrace those others, our empathy becomes stronger. Similarly, our self-control and grit build upon one another, with gains in one area resulting in an improvement in the other. And our integrity is very much relevant to both empathy and embracing diversity because there will invariably come times when we need to take a public stand that runs counter to the majority view.

Moral vs. Performance Character and the Heart/Will/Intellect Model

One helpful way to view SEL skills is through a moral versus performance character perspective: Do the skills refer to an individual's moral character or performance character? Lickona and Davidson (2005) specify that moral character "consists of those qualities—such as integrity, justice, caring, and respect—needed for successful interpersonal relationships and ethical behavior," whereas performance character "consists of

FIGURE 1.1

CASEL's Components of SEL and Related Formative Five Skills

Orientation	Competency	Formative Five Success Skills
Self (intrapersonal intelligence)	Self-awareness: ability to recognize one's emotions	Self-control, integrity
	Self-management: ability to regulate one's emotions	Self-control, integrity, grit
Other (intrapersonal intelligence)	Social awareness: ability to understand others	Empathy, embracing diversity
	Relationship skills: ability to maintain positive relationships with others	Empathy, integrity, embracing diversity
Collaborative (intrapersonal and interpersonal intelligences)	Problem solving: ability to make productive choices and solve problems	Empathy, self-control, integrity, embracing diversity, grit

those qualities—such as effort, diligence, perseverance, a strong work ethic, a positive attitude, ingenuity, and self-discipline—needed to realize one's potential for excellence in academics, co-curricular activities, the workplace, or any other area of endeavor" (p. 18). Among the Formative Five skills, empathy, integrity, and embracing diversity address moral character, and self-control and grit address performance character.

In his 2017 article for *Education Week*, "The Dirt-Encrusted Roots of Social-Emotional Learning," Chester E. Finn Jr. writes: "Though its partisans will contest the point, social-emotional learning does not seem intended to build character in any traditional sense, nor is it aimed at citizenship. It's awash in the self, steeped in the ability to understand one's own emotions, thoughts, values, strengths, and limitations" (p. 22). To Finn's point, to the degree that schools have addressed character in the past, they have largely addressed performance character. Report cards and student assessments frequently focus on work habits and effort, and sometimes students are recognized for their industry and hard work. Unfortunately, developing children's moral character has been primarily

FIGURE 1.2

Other Approaches to Social-Emotional Growth

Organization	Social-Emotional Components
CASEL	• To identify and understand one's own feelings • To accurately read and comprehend emotional states in others • To manage strong emotions and their expression in a constructive manner • To regulate one's own behavior, to develop empathy for others • To establish and maintain relationships
VIA Institute on Character	• Conscientiousness • Agreeableness • Neuroticism • Openness to experience • Extraversion
Committee for Children	• Empathy • Impulse control • Emotion recognition • Emotion management • Communication • Assertiveness • Problem solving
Wallace Foundation	• Cognitive regulation (attention control, inhibitory control, working memory/planning, cognitive flexibility) • Emotional processes (emotion knowledge/expression, emotion/behavior regulation, empathy/perspective-taking) • Social/interpersonal skills (understanding social cues, conflict resolution, prosocial behavior)

delegated to home and religious institutions because pursuing value judgments can be more controversial. It's easy to agree that hard work and tenacity are positives, but it can be more difficult for empathy to be universally accepted because the "others" for whom empathy is being expressed may not be seen by some to be worthy of consideration. It is important to point out that the moral and performance orientations are not in conflict: In virtually every situation, we will draw from skills from both categories.

In "The Five Success Skills Every Student Should Master" I note, "When we think about the future and what skills and understandings our students will need to be successful, we must begin with the end in mind: We want to develop good people. By asking what kind of people we want on our team and in our neighborhood, we will appreciate the need to teach human literacy" (2018b).

In an article for *Educational Leadership*, Angela Duckworth divides SEL into three categories: "interpersonal character strengths of the heart (gratitude, empathy, honesty, social and emotional intelligence); intrapersonal character strengths of will (academic self-control, grit, growth mindset); and intellectual character strengths (curiosity, open-mindedness, intellectual humility, imagination, and creativity)" (McKibben, 2018, p. 47). In her opinion, the interpersonal character strengths are the most important.

Why the Resistance to SEL?

Three factors come together to make it difficult for educators to give sufficient attention to SEL. Our school systems were designed to develop workers and good citizens, so there has always been a natural focus on the three Rs. Indeed, until relatively recently, problems with solutions that required skill in reading, writing, or mathematics could only be done by people, so those skills were essential to success.

Second, endorsing many of the success skills is, by definition, a value judgment. It is hard to imagine a parent not wanting an offspring to express empathy, but what that means and to whom it is shown will vary considerably. Self-control and integrity seem like wonderful qualities (to me, anyway), and I cannot imagine a parent objecting to them being taught once the parents are comfortable with how they are presented. However, diversity is a topic that elicits less consensus, which is why I precede it with "embracing" in *The Formative Five*. Historically, noncognitive skills, or social-emotional learning, have been considered off-limits for public school educators. (This is far less the case in independent schools and, indeed, many of these promote their role in developing character and social skills as a strategy to attract families. That is much easier for them to do because families would not choose to enroll their child in a school unless they supported the values it was promoting.)

Third, even if there is widespread agreement on the merit of a category, (e.g., grit is desirable), some people feel that this is a skill or an attitude that should be taught at home or, possibly, through a religious institution, and not addressed in school.

Our reluctance to focus on nonscholastic areas is due, in large part, to the fact that they are more subjective than traditional subjects. But that should not deter us.

My Journey to SEL Advocacy

Though I am now a fierce proponent of SEL, my undergraduate education program focused solely on preparing me to teach traditional subject matter—basically, the three Rs. When I graduated, I was well prepared to teach these areas, but that was it. I don't recall any time being devoted to teaching children how to live and work with others. Of course, simply from working in classrooms, educators were aware of vast differences among children in terms of who would work well with others, who was caring, who could persevere, and so on, but we viewed these differences in the same way that we viewed height or weight: We assumed they were due to genetics and how kids were raised at home. We were trained to teach academics to students, and we didn't see ourselves as having much involvement with these other areas. Based on many conversations and e-mail exchanges I've had since, I suspect that quite a few readers have traveled a similar path.

That narrow focus on academics continued when I began teaching. I met with my first principal in August, a couple of weeks prior to the beginning of school, and he gave me the teachers' guides to all the textbooks I would be using in my 5th grade classroom. We did not discuss any other aspect of children's growth.

I knew that the school to which I was assigned was in a dangerous area—on the first day of class, I even had my car stolen. (On the plus side, I told myself, things could only get better from there.) Unsurprisingly, it was an underachieving school, and today it is clear to me that quite a few of my students would have had high Adverse Childhood Experience (ACE) scores, indicating that they had experienced stressful or traumatic events that could lead to social and health problems (see Anda, n.d.). Students with higher ACE scores also often have difficulties in school. Of course, the ACE construct was not known at the time I started teaching. (You can learn more about ACE scores here: www.preventchildabuse.org/images/docs/anda_wht_ppr.pdf.)

Establishing and maintaining discipline was a major issue at the school because students' inattention and misbehaviors routinely interfered with their learning. Almost all our principal's and teachers' efforts went to establishing clear and strict consequences for misbehavior, with little or no attention given to teaching and developing nonacademic qualities in our students. When my principal talked about achievement and growth, it was always in terms of students' standardized test results—period. (Remember the fate of poor Sam Suedo?)

I saw many students at the school who struggled academically but who also displayed qualities that would make them ideal employees and neighbors. Many of the same 5th graders who found writing an essay or solving a complex math problem to be a challenge were also extraordinarily hard-working, caring, responsible, and honest. No doubt you have had students like this, too. I knew that their writing and math skills needed to improve, but I also knew that their strengths in these other areas should be developed and applauded, even if the district's report card gave me little opportunity to do that.

My experiences teaching at this school for a few years, teaching at another school in the suburbs, and leading two very different schools only confirmed for me the necessity of addressing these nonacademic skills. Every year, I was struck by the difference between the categories on students' report cards—what, by definition, we said was important in school and what I knew was important in life.

The need to focus on what is truly important has been reflected in many of the "Principal Connection" columns I've written for *Educational Leadership*. For example, my 2008/2009 column "Data That Count" begins with a comment that a parent said to me: "If you can't measure it, then it doesn't matter." He was arguing for the importance of standardized tests and expressing concern because his daughter had only done very well and not exceptionally well, as he had expected. In responding to him, I noted, "What standardized tests cannot do—indeed, what almost no test can do—is capture a child's essence. Tests don't speak to the internal factors that play a major role in life success: curiosity, effort, resilience, and compassion." (You can see the column here: www.ascd.org/publications/educational-leadership/dec08/vol66/num04/Data-That-Count.aspx.) I specifically address additional aspects of SEL and the Formative Five success skills in the following other "Principal Connection" columns:

- "Got Grit?" (2012)—"As educators, part of our job is to ensure that every child finds success, and an important part of finding success is knowing how to respond to failure." (www.ascd.org/publications/educational-leadership/mar12/vol69/num06/Got-Grit%C2%A2.aspx)

- "Why You Need a Diversity Champion" (2016)—"If you assume that everyone at your school realizes diversity is important, so it doesn't need a formal champion—you're wrong. It's precisely because affirming all the aspects of each child's identity is so important to growth and development that diversity needs a point person." (www.ascd.org/publications/educational-leadership/apr16/vol73/num07/Why-You-Need-a-Diversity-Champion.aspx)

- "Building Empathy in Schools" (2018a)—"Too many people are quick to judge and even to call names. Our schools aren't immune to trends in society, and chances are that these rancorous attitudes have seeped into your school. It's probably obvious in both the student cafeteria and at faculty meetings." (www.ascd. org/publications/educational-leadership/apr18/vol75/num07/ Building-Empathy-in-Schools.aspx)

Social-Emotional Coaches

Perhaps the best evidence that SEL is becoming recognized as an essential aspect of education is that schools and school districts are beginning to employ SEL coaches. I first heard about these positions at a recent ASCD conference, tweeted a request for more information, and received many responses. It was encouraging to hear that so many schools and districts are creating positions designed to support students' SEL. The kinds of schools and where these positions are lodged in the districts' hierarchies vary, but in every situation, the SEL coach is designed to be a support for teachers. Dana Januszka, who worked with school districts in her role as an SEL coach for the University of Delaware, puts it simply: The role of the SEL coach, she says, is to "teach people how to build relationships and talk to kids." Lisa Maher, SEL support specialist at Parker Elementary School in Billerica, Massachusetts, notes: "My goal was for the teachers to see me as a partner, someone who could support them and help them to be more effective in reaching their students' SEL needs."

Building a trusting relationship with staff is an essential part of being an SEL coach. Although the interactions of SEL coaches with classroom teachers are similar to those of literacy and mathematics coaches, the nature of SEL requires an even deeper and more trusting relationship. "These relationships are far more personal," says Krista Leh of Resonance Educational Consulting. "In order to most effectively foster SEL growth in students, educators need to be able to look inward to assess their own SEL development and competencies." Emmie Pawlak, director of teaching and learning for the Keeneyville (Illinois) Schools, where a SEL Curriculum Committee meets every four or five weeks, agrees: "SEL is a curriculum, and the coaches' relationships with teachers requires vulnerability by everyone. Our coaches don't evaluate, but work with teachers as colleagues."

SEL coaches collaborate with classroom teachers to plan lessons, brainstorm strategies for students (and their parents), provide feedback, and review classroom and schoolwide procedures. It's important to consider, for example, "Do our disciplinary structures support SEL?" asks Rachelle Finck, the Coordinator of SEL for the Round Rock ISD in Texas. Reviewing both formal and informal curriculum is vital for the implementation of any successful SEL program.

At the Michael R. Hollis Innovation Academy in Atlanta, Georgia, teachers celebrate SEL skills by addressing them through memorable schoolwide events. The SEL coach position at the academy, a K–7 school of 700 students, is held by Dennis Toliver. In addition to working with new-to-the-school teachers before the start of school and all teachers throughout the year, he is responsible for Hollis's monthly schoolwide community meetings. "These are positively-oriented sessions designed to talk about the habits we want students to develop," he says. Each month, a student from every grade is celebrated as a "Hollis Hero" for embodying one of the school's SEL habits: self-discipline, collaboration, creativity, communication, empathy, and perseverance. Rubrics have been created for each grade to help students understand what each habit entails. Toliver says that he works with the teachers to try to ensure that as many different students as possible can be recognized. Occasionally, students from Spelman and Morehouse Colleges join the meeting to speak and perform a step-show.

Erin Schulte, the coordinator of curriculum, counseling, and character education for the Parkway (Missouri) School District, emphasizes the following SEL skills in schools: noble purpose/love, humility, courage, gratitude, forgiveness, empowerment, foresight, and stewardship (Berkowitz, Bier, & McCauley, 2016). Her district has a Character Education Action Team that focuses on promoting values. Michael Barolak, director of social emotional support services for the district, supervises four social-emotional behavior specialists (SEBs) and defines their mission as changing mindsets by examining problems through an SEL lens.

Effectively working with teachers is integral to the position, so his advice to the SEBs is to "find the allies in your building."

Devin Quinlan, the behavior and wellness coach at Missisquoi Valley High School in Swanton, Vermont, says that most of his work with teachers and students takes place outside classrooms. The school has a monthly meeting focused on SEL in which faculty members are divided into groups of 10, each with 2 facilitators. Quinlan provides leadership by suggesting and summarizing articles on SEL best practices and leading an effort to create case studies based on actual students so that faculty members can create sound SEL guidelines. Because it is a new role, Quinlan is working to develop a culture in which teachers are open to going to him for ideas and support. He shares that he often plays the role of mediator, following up with students on their efforts to improve their SEL. Occasionally he also plays the role of disciplinarian, but he always ensures that students understand that their consequences stem from a behavior, not from anything inherent—and strives always to do so with dignity.

What's Ahead?

I believe that as important as the Formative Five skills have been in the past, they will be even more essential in the future. "What seems increasingly evident is that the primary condition of the network era is not just rapid change, but constant change," write Ito and Howe in *Whiplash* (2016). How much time do you spend on e-mail each day? How often do you check Google, for example? (I suspect a quick and valid response to both questions is "too much.") Through the internet and especially social media, we are routinely connected with hundreds, thousands, maybe millions of people we have never met in person.

Already, this has created shifts in how relationships are formed and maintained. In his book *The Complacent Class* (2017), Tyler Cowen notes that more than a third of couples married between 2005 and 2012 met online—and this was the case for almost 70 percent of same-sex couples. According to Common Sense Media, teenagers average nine hours a day online (2015). As people become increasingly adept at interacting with others in virtual reality, we must ensure that the skills required to build relationships with people in the same room don't fall by the wayside. In his article "What Google Learned from Its Quest to Build the Perfect Team," Charles Duhigg notes that "effective teams are characterized by equal participation among the group members and a sensitivity to one another's words and actions"—practices for which SEL skills are paramount. He goes on to say that the effective teams he studied "all had high 'average social sensitivity'—a fancy way of saying they were skilled at intuiting how others felt based on their tone of voice, their expressions, and other nonverbal cues" (2016). (Other studies have noted that this empathic interpersonal sensitivity—the ability to read and understand others—is relevant when collaborating online, too!)

Technology is also leading to a huge shift in the kinds of jobs for which we need to prepare students. For example, Walmart has automated such tasks as scrubbing floors, unloading trucks, and monitoring inventory—all tasks that were once the full-time domain of human beings. Jobs that require training and certification will also change: According to *Business Insider*, self-driving trucks will be the norm within the next decade, putting at risk an estimated 3 million truck driving jobs (Premack, 2018). What will happen to them as well as to the thousands of people who work in truck stops and roadside motels? Technological advances will affect every sector of life and work. In the 2018 *New York Times* article "Meet Zora, The Robot Caregiver," authors Satariano, Peltier, and Kostyukov (2018) introduce us to a robot named Zora that is being used in France as a companion for people living in senior facilities. "Many patients developed an emotional attachment, treating it like a baby, holding and cooing, giving it kisses on the head," they write (p. B1). "Giving robots more responsibility to care for people in the twilight of their life may seem like a dystopian prospect, but many see it as an inevitability" (p. B4).

"[T]he highest-paying jobs in the future will be *stempathy* jobs," writes Thomas Friedman in *Thank You for Being Late* (2016)—"jobs that combine strong science and technological skills with the ability to empathize with another human being" (p. 450). The process is already underway in the medical industry: Researchers at Massachusetts General Hospital (2019) have found that "virtual video visits . . . can successfully replace office visits for many patients without compromising the quality of care and communication." I wonder how long it will be until we describe a doctor's SEL by referring to his or her *screenside* manner!

Perhaps the simplest way to phrase the importance of SEL to the future of our students comes from Ingeborg Van Teeseling in her 2019 article "How Are We Going to Teach Our Kids to Be Balanced People If We Aren't?" She writes, "Jobs then will not just be focused on technology, but on a blend of technology and AI, robotics and a whole lot of other things that we can only dream of now. The key to this brave new world is communication, and people who can make connections to other people will be the masters of the universe."

About This Book

This book shows how educators can leverage school culture to implement social-emotional learning, develop student character, and cultivate the Formative Five success skills in the classroom. Chapter 2 describes the Formative Five success skills in action. Chapter 3 discusses what culture is, followed by chapters on the five essential components of school culture: Vision, Mission, Values (Chapter 4), Practices (Chapter 5), People (Chapter 6), Narrative (Chapter 7), and Place (Chapter 8). Leadership—by people in all roles—is discussed in Chapter 9, and Chapter 10 offers my conclusions and suggestions.

In the pages that follow you'll find many examples from educators and schools as well as suggestions of my own drawn from personal experiences. I am confident that this book will be a valuable resource to many people. I know that I learned a great deal from writing it.

2

The Formative Five
Success Skills

I am an observer. I'm the guy who notices where people sit at meetings, who makes a mental note of who speaks up first, who's reticent, and who talks often. I watch how others react and with whom people gather during a break or at recess. I note how people approach a task, whether they want to work alone or prefer to work in a group, and who takes a leadership role. For decades I have seen people grow and succeed in a range of settings. Sometimes this was surprising, and sometimes not. I wondered what qualities and behaviors related to who succeeded where.

I have taught in city and suburban elementary schools, been an adjunct professor at two universities, coached athletic teams, and led public and private schools. I've seen students I first knew as 5-year-old children grow up and become parents, community activists, teachers, physicians, artists, attorneys, salespeople, administrators, and veterinarians. I've also worked with scores of educators and seen teachers and principals taking risks, gaining new knowledge, developing skills, and finding new ways to help students learn.

Although these settings, the individuals, and my roles varied considerably, there was one commonality. In each of these experiences, it became very clear to me that the people who advanced toward a goal were able to do so primarily because of their interpersonal and intrapersonal qualities—and especially from what I call the Formative Five success skills of *empathy, self-control, integrity, embracing diversity,* and *grit.* Following are some real-life examples of these skills in action.

Empathy

Mrs. Knight was an excellent teacher known for her strict and effective behavioral expectations. She was fond of saying, with a bit of a laugh, "In my room, it's my way or the highway!" Her class was one of structure, order, and compliance. Her students quickly learned the classroom rules and complied with them. To Mrs. Knight, *flexibility* was just a word in the dictionary, but her students understood that she cared about them and they almost always left her class with fond memories. As the principal, I valued Mrs. Knight's strengths, recognizing that while her style wasn't always what I would have preferred, students grew and prospered in her classroom, and that is what mattered. I was quite cognizant of which students would do well with Mrs. Knight and which ones would find her especially challenging.

One year, Juan, a student with a number of personal issues, enrolled in Mrs. Knight's class. Juan's parents were upfront about his difficulties, and ours was the third school in which he would enroll in three years. In retrospect, his behaviors indicated that he was on the Asperger's continuum, although we were not aware of that term at the time. I worried whether Mrs. Knight's classroom was the right setting for him, but there was no other option; her class had the only available vacancy. Juan was extremely bright, but he displayed many of the behaviors that drive teachers to frustration. He was rigid and linear in his understanding, often misinterpreting or overlooking nuances. He was obsessive yet careless, resistant to authority, and not very social. His behaviors, as well as his unrealized potential, had frustrated him and his teachers to the point where Juan no longer wanted to go to school (and I suspect that the teachers were pleased not to have him in their class).

School began and I held my breath, but by the end of the first week it was clear that Mrs. Knight's class was a wonderful place for Juan.

He loved being in her room, wanted to come to school, and performed much better than ever before. That's because rather than simply trying to get Juan to conform to her approach and expectations, and despite her reputation for being inflexible, Mrs. Knight worked to understand his challenges. Once she saw his records and met with his parents, Mrs. Knight knew that Juan would need some extra attention. She wanted to know how he reacted in different situations and how he perceived his environment. During the first day of school, she pulled Juan aside to meet privately with him. "I care about you and I know you're bright," she said, "so help me understand why school is so difficult. What frustrates or is hard for you?"

Mrs. Knight told me later that Juan seemed a bit surprised that she asked these questions, and he was very open with her about what things bothered him. During the first week of school, Mrs. Knight made a point of meeting with Juan each morning to give him a hug and tell him that it would be a good day, and then again at the end of the day to see how the day had gone and what he was feeling. Her desire to know Juan and her willingness to listen set the tone for them to build a positive relationship. Over the course of the year, she watched and listened to Juan intently, meeting regularly with him to learn how he was feeling. She learned his frustrations and could anticipate most difficult situations and help him avoid them, and he learned to trust her. Theirs was not always an easy relationship, but at the end of the year, Juan said that the best year of his life was being in Mrs. Knight's class, and his parents agreed.

Self-Control

Known by all to be an amazing teacher, Mr. Deiter was not a very organized person. You only needed to look at his desk to appreciate the depth of his disorganization. It was filled with piles of paper, stacks of books, family photos (largely obscured by the papers), pens and pencils, several bottles of water, and sticky notes containing scribbled messages placed on just about everything. In fact, there were sticky notes stuck on other sticky notes. On the floor were more stacks of paper, several piles of books (some precariously high), more than a dozen sets of three-by-five cards held together by rubber bands, and a shoebox overflowing with protractors and compasses. He collected seashells and Chicago Cubs artifacts, and these were displayed on just about every flat surface. These collections were as much a part of Mr. Deiter's identity as were the wild ties he wore each day. Altogether, the area resembled the interior of a filled-to-bursting storeroom.

Mr. Deiter's class was popular. Students wanted to be assigned to his classroom, were eager to come to school, and learned a great deal. Mr. Deiter's plan book was filled with big- and small-print items as well as notes, asterisks, underlines, and the URLs to content-related websites. The lessons and interactions in his classroom almost seemed choreographed; it was obvious that despite all the clutter, planning and organization were essential to Mr. Deiter's success. You see, Mr. Deiter had a strong intrapersonal intelligence and was very self-aware. He knew that his penchant for disorganization and collecting (two sides of the same coin) would interfere with his teaching unless he controlled it, so control it he did.

There was a huge old-fashioned schoolhouse clock hanging on the wall in the front of Mr. Deiter's classroom, and each day's schedule was written on the whiteboard next to it. All the days' activities were completed according to the schedule—down to the minute. Students were assigned seats on the bus for field trips. Mr. Deiter began each class by meeting with groups of students so that they could report on their homework progress and review their goals for the day. At 3 p.m. his wristwatch alarm would go off to remind him to check with these groups.

Mr. Deiter spent time at the beginning of every year teaching his students how to organize their desks, arrange the supplies in their lockers, and follow the rules for submitting homework assignments. He also reviewed these procedures on the first day of school after winter and spring breaks. Students in Mr. Deiter's class set individual academic and personal goals, planned strategies, and reported on their progress weekly. At the end of the year, the students shared their goal progress with their parents. Though you wouldn't have imagined it by seeing his desk, Mr. Deiter's planning and structure helped make his classroom one in which all students succeeded.

Integrity

Ms. Lallie's class was one of traditions. She was an excellent teacher, and she was known most to her students and their parents for bringing her personal passions to the classroom—by teaching about President Lincoln, for example, and about knitting. Each year featured a play written by students that covered some aspect of Lincoln's life and a voluntary knitting club at recess that most of Ms. Lallie's students attended. Tales about these activities were handed down from student to student.

Ms. Lallie's reputation as a superb teacher was held far and wide in the community, but among her peers, she was recognized for another trait: She was a person of strong convictions who was never reluctant to share her beliefs. She was a fierce advocate for students and outspoken about protecting the rights of staff members. Teachers knew that she would be comfortable pushing against the grain or making a statement that would not be popular with the administration (that would be me) or, occasionally, with her colleagues. As a result, she was someone to whom other teachers would turn if they were reluctant to voice a dissenting opinion or concern; they hoped she could be their voice. Sometimes in a committee meeting, I could see teachers subtly turning to her and waiting, hoping that she would make the recusant comment that was on the tip of their tongues.

Among parents, too, Ms. Lallie earned a reputation for candor. Because parents knew that she cared about their children, they would listen as she told them what she thought they needed to hear, no matter how serious or difficult it was. One year, a very well-connected parent in the community stopped in to see me after his parent-teacher conference with Ms. Lallie. "I must tell you," he said, "I admire her courage. I didn't want to hear what she told me, but I am glad I did." I asked him what had happened. "She told me that 5th grade is a year of ups and downs for students, especially boys," he said. "They become interested in the other sex, and hormones are beginning to pop. Then she said, 'Well, I'm sure the second half of the year will have lots of ups because your son has started off with quite a few downs,' and we both laughed."

It might be natural to assume that Ms. Lallie was comfortable speaking out because she had earned a gravitas from her fine teaching and strong reputation. However, Ms. Lallie's outspokenness was part of her from the day she entered our school. She spoke out and played the iconoclast role before she had "earned" it because standing up for her beliefs was simply her identity. Once, after a particularly contentious discussion with a colleague, she said to me, "I have to stand up for what I believe is right, even if it turns out that I am wrong."

Sure, there were times when Ms. Lallie caused me to count to 10 or reach for a Tylenol, and there were occasions when I wished that she was a bit more go-along-to-get-along. But I recognized the value that her voice brought to the school and to me. She often said things that I needed to hear even if I didn't want to, and her courage reminded all of us that we need to visibly act and speak for our beliefs. We were a better school because of her.

Embracing Diversity

"If some of our African American families are uncomfortable because they don't feel that our halls reflect their presence and value," said Mr. Wallace, "then we'll know we are successful when some of our white families complain that they don't see themselves on the walls." He was a member of the board of directors and a very successful white business-man. We had just heard a presentation by an African American mom who felt that a midnight stroll through our school's halls would not give the impression that diversity was important at our school when it certainly was. We valued diversity highly at our school, but that value wasn't reflected in what was posted on the walls.

A discussion among board members, teachers, and administrators ensued. It wasn't easy because some people were slow to see the power of signage and symbols, but eventually we reached a consensus that the halls and walls should shout our values for all to hear. Mr. Wallace's comment about making it a goal to create some discomfort among the power group was met with many nods and a few smiles. As the school's leader, I took great encouragement from this license. Mr. Wallace's comment reflected the reality that change does not come without a cost; if you want to make an omelet, you have to break a few eggs.

Ms. Spears understood that causing discomfort was part of her role as director of diversity and inclusion at our school. "I'm an equal opportunity dis-comforter," she said to me once. "My role is to push diversity issues in such a way that everyone experiences some discomfort." She chaired the monthly meetings of our faculty diversity committee; supported our parent diversity committee, which met in the evenings five or six times per year; coordinated our parent affinity groups for parents of color, parents of adopted children, and gay and lesbian families; and led us in professional development diversity activities. During one August inservice training, Ms. Spears had faculty engage in an online activity designed to educate us about social biases, beginning with those that we ourselves hold. Images flash on a screen and participants share their visceral reactions to them. Some of us were chagrined to learn about our biases (e.g., that we were more likely to assume a person of color was the miscreant even though a white guy held the pistol). The tests, created by Project Implicit, are available for a range of diversity-related issues. (More information can be found here: https://implicit.harvard .edu/implicit/selectatest.html.)

The faculty diversity committee read books such as Ta-Nehisi Coates's *Between the World and Me* (2015), Tim Wise's *White Like Me* (2004), and Eddie Moore Jr., Ali Michael, and Marguerite W. Penick-Parks's *The Guide for White Women Who Teach Black Boys* (2018), as well as many articles, to gain insights on and further discuss issues of race, class, and gender. Going beyond working with the faculty, Ms. Spears led us in reaching into our community after Michael Brown was killed in nearby Ferguson, Missouri. Three weeks after his death, we hosted a forum in our school's theater. Attended by staff, parents, and some neighbors, the evening opened with a panel discussion of race from different perspectives (see Hoerr,

2015). After this, the audience met in small groups to generate strategies for individual action to reduce racism in our society. (More on the event can be found here: www.ascd.org/publications/educational-leadership/mar15/vol72/num06/Responding-to-Ferguson.aspx.)

Teachers knew that they could go to Ms. Spears for ideas about how to handle just about any diversity-related issue. Her actions showed that diversity at our school truly was more than the demographics of our students and staff ("diversity beyond the numbers" was part of our slogan). Rather, we actively embraced diversity by consciously creating discussions and activities that increased understanding of others. The importance of having someone on staff like Ms. Spears who takes the responsibility for pushing diversity forward can't be undersold. I talk more about this in my April 2016 column for *Educational Leadership*, "Why You Need a Diversity Champion" (found here: www.ascd.org/publications/educational-leadership/apr16/vol73/num07/Why-You-Need-a-Diversity-Champion.aspx).

Grit

Mr. Oats was a principal whom I knew quite well. We would meet periodically to share observations and ideas about personnel issues, curriculum, and life. These meetings began when he first became a principal (he previously was an assistant principal at another school) and continued for many years, growing into a strong friendship. I was able to witness his evolution as a leader by hearing his challenges, responses to challenges, and rationales for his responses. I saw him grow in many ways, and I also saw how his school benefitted from his leadership.

The formula for Mr. Oats's success seemed obvious. Known for his constant smile and positive attitude, he was a beloved figure—as beloved as a principal can be, anyway—and was respected by everyone. It was easy to see why: He was in constant motion, visiting classrooms, chatting with students in the halls or at lunch, even teaching a class each semester. Through just a brief conversation, it became clear that Mr. Oats was a hard worker, highly knowledgeable, and student-centered. These same skills and positive qualities also came across very loudly when he and I would meet at coffee shops.

But as a friend and observer, someone with whom Mr. Oats had candidly shared his hopes, plans, and thoughts, I saw something else that set him apart: Mr. Oats never gave up on an issue. When he was frustrated or failed, he would step back, reflect, and then plan how to move forward. He would review, reflect, and reframe, and then redo the process again. When Mr. Oats latched on to an issue that he thought was important for students and his school, there was no stopping him; he lived the passion-plus-perseverance formula known as grit.

Grit was a part of Mr. Oats's identity. When we first met, I asked him to tell me about his experiences as a teacher and assistant principal and to describe some of his achievements. "What did you do well and what did you learn?" I asked. In reflecting on his teacher and principal roles, he talked about connecting with some hard-to-reach students, and he also talked about being in charge of curriculum and student-con-duct reform efforts at his previous school. He wasn't boastful, but it was clear that he had led the school in making significant strides forward. It was also obvious that each of these gains were due to his tenacity. He cared deeply about his students and the school, and he was committed to teacher development and growth; that's the passion part of grit. Mr. Oats never, ever gave up. The curriculum reform effort, for example, took three years to complete, and Mr. Oats told me that there were numerous roadblocks, including a group of senior teachers who resisted anything that might compromise their autonomy. But he was never deterred; he would regroup, pause, plot another strategy, and push forward again. His personality and intellect were very strong, but it was his grit that enabled him to succeed.

Note: Mrs. Knight, Mr. Deiter, Ms. Lallie, Ms. Spears, and Mr. Oats are composites of people with whom I worked, from whom I learned, and about whom I cared.

Defining the Formative Five

As you read about Mrs. Knight, Mr. Deiter, Ms. Lallie, Ms. Spears, Mr. Wallace, and Mr. Oats, were you reminded of people you know or with whom you have worked? I suspect that this is the case even though you may not have used the exact same terms to describe them. Each of the Formative Five skills can be addressed by a variety of other terms, as shown in Figure 2.1.

FIGURE 2.1

Other Terms for the Formative Five

Success Skills	Some Other Associated Terms
Empathy	Caring, understanding, compassionate
Self-control	Measured, restrained, disciplined
Integrity	Honest, trustworthy, respectful
Embracing Diversity	Tolerant, accepting, culturally responsive
Grit	Tenacious, resilient, fortitude

Source: From *The Formative Five: Fostering Grit, Empathy, and Other Success Skills Every Student Needs* (p. 11), by T. R. Hoerr, 2017, Alexandria, VA: ASCD. Copyright 2017 by ASCD.

Following are detailed descriptions of each of the Formative Five skills.

Empathy

"Empathy is the capacity to accurately understand the position of others—to feel that 'this could happen to me,'" writes J. D. Trout (2009, p. 21). To Simon Baron-Cohen, "empathy, itself, is the most valuable resource in the world" (2011, p. 107). German theologian Dietrich Bonhomie defines empathy as "the view from below . . . the ability to see great events of world history . . . from the perspective of the outcast, the suspects, the maltreated, the powerless, the reviled—in short, from the perspective of those who suffer" (cited in Koehn, 2017, p. 294).

Though I don't wish to place the Formative Five skills in a hierarchy, I always like to discuss empathy first because I think it is sorely lacking in today's society. Whether it's in the harshness of public comments at a school board meeting, conveyed by the facial expressions of someone impatiently waiting in line, or vividly displayed in the rhetoric at a political rally, we see and feel a lack of empathy so often that it has become routine, almost acceptable.

In virtually every sector, our voices and lack of appreciation for others' perspectives are more strident today than they were in the past. This unwillingness to see issues from another's perspective crosses political boundaries and hierarchical positions. Indeed, in *These Truths* (2018), Jill Lepore notes "Between 1958 and 2015, the proportion of Americans who told pollsters that they 'basically trust the government' fell from 73 percent to 19 percent" (p. 726). Writing in *Psychology Today*, Maia Szalavitz (2010) references a study of 14,000 college students showing that those enrolling in colleges after 2000 "have empathy levels that are 40 [percent] lower than those who came before them." Too often, tolerance—even taking the time to visibly listen to an opposing viewpoint— is portrayed as weakness.

No doubt the pervasiveness of technology has played a significant role in the decline of empathy. According to CBS News, children ages 8 to 18 "spend an average of more than seven hours a day looking at screens" (Welch, 2018), in contrast to the American Heart Association's recommendation of two hours a day, and one hour per day for children ages 2 to 5 (2018). Lepore notes that "social media had provided a breeding ground for fanaticism, authoritarianism, and nihilism" (2018, p. 770), and Aisha Sultan (2018) writes in the *St. Louis Post-Dispatch* that the "growing empathy deficit may be fueled by several factors, including isolation by social class and chronic stress." Clearly, our obligation to teach our students empathy has never been stronger.

In *Mama's Last Hug: Animal Emotions and What They Tell Us About Ourselves* (2019), Frans de Waal writes that "[e]mpathic reactions are always stronger the more we have in common with [others] and the closer we feel to them" (p. 96), further noting that *emotional contagion,* as this sense of closeness is known, begins at birth when one baby cries upon hearing another baby cry. "To respond empathetically," writes Michelle Borba, "kids must see themselves as people who care and value others' thoughts and feelings" (2016, p. 41).

From kindergarten up, empathy is a word that should be part of everyone's vocabulary and used routinely. Posters and signs proclaiming the definition of empathy and offering some visual examples should pervade the school. (This is true for each of the success skills.) Students need to intentionally pursue empathy by working to hear and understand others' experiences, perspectives, and feelings, and by engaging in activities that stem from these understandings.

These steps are reflected in a categorization by Paul Ekman, noted by Daniel Goleman (2007):

1. *Cognitive empathy:* knowing what the other person feels. Receptive learning comes from gathering information, learning about others' situations and perspectives.
2. *Emotional empathy:* feeling what the other person feels. This comes from interactions with those others—seeing, hearing, maybe meeting them—to understand and appreciate their feelings.
3. *Actionable empathy:* acting from knowing what the other person feels (termed "compassionate empathy" by Goleman). Engaged efforts to help others leads to generative learning, creating new knowledge and opportunities.

As we will see in subsequent chapters, the success skills are best taught when students are active learners. Students need to formally learn about empathy in lessons and from books; they need to interact with others, talking and learning from them; and they need to participate in outreach or activities that stem from their understanding. Designing learning in a way that addresses receptive, interactive, and generative learning styles (see Figure 2.2) not only benefits students but also provides opportunities for teachers to engage and learn.

FIGURE 2.2
Levels of Empathy and Associated Results, Learning Styles, and Student Outcomes

Level of Empathy	Result	Learning Style	Student Outcomes
Cognitive empathy	Knowing the other person's feelings	Receptive	Student explains others' situations and perspectives
Emotional empathy	Holding the other person's feelings	Interactive	Student has emotions that correspond with these situations and perspectives
Actionable empathy	Acting from your empathy	Generative	Student takes action to support others

Gaining empathy can have a profound and positive effect on behavior. De Waal (2019) offers an example: "Within days after a good friend of mine broke his leg, his dog started dragging her own. In both cases, it was the right leg. The dog's limp lasted for weeks but vanished miraculously once my friend's cast came off" (p. 93). Similarly, I have seen teachers become strong advocates for specific social justice efforts because they worked closely with children who needed this particular kind of support. In subsequent chapters, we will see how a school's culture can help every child—and every adult—become more empathic.

Self-Control

American humorist Will Rogers once said, "The road to success is dotted with many tempting parking spaces." Much has changed since Will Rogers's time, but the presence of temptations remains. Whether it's eating that second dessert or watching *The Good Place* instead of grading papers, we are constantly being tempted by opportunities that aren't the best use of our time or energies.

Those who succeed most in life possess the self-control to avoid falling for these traps. Self-control incorporates many attitudes: focus, restraint, patience, optimism. People with strong self-control can ignore distractions, count to 3 or 33 before responding impetuously, recognize that the goal is a long way away, and remain confident that they will succeed. Nobel-winning economist James Heckman notes that characteristics of self-control such as "strength of motivation, an ability to act on long-term plans, and the social-emotional regulation needed to work with others . . . also have a large impact on earnings, employment, labor force experience, college attendance, teenage pregnancy, participation in risky activities, compliance with health protocols, and participation in crime" (2013, p. 12).

Self-control is hard for most people, but our habits are changeable. In *The Power of Habit* (2012), Charles Duhigg talks about making (or breaking) habits by first examining the cues that cause us to act in a certain way. Then we can establish new patterns with rewards that serve as incentives, and consciously work to form them into a habit. He notes that the chance of intentionally forming a habit increases if it "grows out of a communal experience, even if that community is only as large as two people" (p. 93).

As educators, we can use the power of the group to help students develop self-control. One way is to have students use the chart in Figure 2.3, which includes a column for listing collaborators in addition to academic and personal self-control goals. By setting both types of goals, we increase the possibility of transferring habits from one area to the other. Obstacles and distractions should be anticipated and noted so that plans can be made to surmount them. Collaborators could include both children and adults, students and staff members. They could help students develop goals and strategies or meet with them regularly to share progress, brainstorm new strategies, and offer support. The final column asks how success will be ascertained. There can be power in envisioning success and sharing this vision with peers.

FIGURE 2.3
Self-Control Strategies and Goals

	Goal	Obstacles/ Distractions	Collaborators	How Success Is Defined
Academic Goal				
Personal Goal				

Walter Mischel's famous Marshmallow Test generated much public awareness about the issue of self-control. Four-year-old children who were sitting alone in a room were offered one marshmallow and told by a researcher that they could receive a second one if they could wait for 15 minutes without eating the first one. The researcher then exited the room and the children were left to their own devices. Some kids ate the marshmallow immediately (that would have been me), while others tried a range of strategies to enforce their self-control, from ignoring the marshmallow to playing with it and even turning it into a racing car. A longitudinal study of these children, comparing those who ate the marshmallow against those who were able to wait, showed significant differences in the two groups over time. In *Emotional Intelligence* (1995), Goleman notes that the students who waited the 15 minutes before eating the first marshmallow scored an average of 210 points higher on their SAT tests 14 years later than did their peers. But higher test scores are only a piece of the benefits. "The more seconds they waited at age four or five," writes Mischel, "the higher their SAT scores and the better their rated social and cognitive functioning in adolescence. At age 27–32, those who had waited longer during the Marshmallow Test in preschool had a lower body mass index and a better sense of self-worth, pursued their goals more effectively, and coped more adaptively with frustration and stress. At midlife, those who could consistently wait ('high delay'), versus those who couldn't ('low delay'), were characterized by distinctively different brain scans in areas linked to addictions and obe-sity" (2014, p. 5).

The Marshmallow Test resonates because of its simplicity and implications. However, we also need to consider factors that may vitiate its power. For example, the prospect of waiting to get a second marsh-mallow may not appeal to a child who has learned that adults cannot be trusted. Why take a chance on waiting for a second marshmallow when it may not appear? For that matter, why risk the marshmallow you already have by waiting to eat it? And what many would assume is simply a marshmallow may, in fact, be an exotic treat if a child isn't used to it.

It is important to note that self-control isn't hereditary. "The tradi-tional belief that willpower is an inborn trait that you either have a lot of or you don't (but cannot do much about it either way) is false," writes Mischel. "Instead, self-control skills, both cognitive and emotional, can be learned, enhanced, and harnessed so that they become automatically activated when you need them" (2014, p. 230).

Integrity

We show our integrity through our visible behaviors. It is a public statement, made with or without words.

When I was first choosing the skills that would become the Forma-tive Five, I strongly considered including *honesty* as one of them. After all, who could be against honesty? It is an integral component of trust, the building block of any relationship, so of course it would be a foun-dational success skill. And doesn't every teacher begin the first day and first class by talking about the importance of honesty, from owning up to errors to only submitting your own work to responding truthfully when asked a question?

Although honesty is important—and it very much is!—it is just a beginning. Whether our goal is to live and work in an effective and healthy setting or whether it is to make the world a better place, integrity is essential. In contrast to being honest, integrity is manifested by taking a public stand and doing the right thing for others to see. Honesty is typically an instinctual reaction, whereas integrity is a conscious choice that often requires courage. As Brené Brown puts it in *Dare to Lead*, "Integrity is practicing your values, not just professing them" (2018, p. 227). Figure 2.4 shows characteristics of honesty versus integrity.

FIGURE 2.4
Honesty Versus Integrity

Behavior	Private	Public	Honesty	Integrity
Discerning	X		X	
Acting/Responding	X		X	
Saying Openly		X		X
Initiating/Creating		X		X
Acting Visibly		X		X

We see the leadership aspect of integrity in action when taking a public stand is designed to influence others. Howard Gardner refers to this when he says that "as one gets older, it does not suffice to keep one's own ethical house in order. One acquires a responsibility over broader realms of which one is a member" (2006, p. 23). This isn't easy. We all want to be accepted by others, yet our integrity requires that we point out an injustice even—especially—if the larger group accepts it. Our integrity requires us to act on our discomfort when things are wrong. "Integrity compels us to be socially conscious and other-directed, and to welcome both personal and professional responsibility," notes Barbara Killinger. "Its values encourage us to be honest in all our dealings and committed to a lifelong search for truth and justice. Its influence empowers us to be understanding rather than judgmental" (2010, p. 13). We often must push against injustice, entropy, gimcrack solutions, and others' perceptions, and our integrity enables us to follow our values and our conscience.

Integrity is closely related to the other Formative Five success skills. Here's how:

- We act upon the *empathy* we feel for others, regardless of whether this sentiment is shared by our peers. Example: A teacher makes a point of eating lunch with his high school students who had fallen into disfavor with his colleagues.

- We display *self-control* even if this means saying no when everyone around us yells "YES!" Example: Years ago, the mother of one of my students told me how proud she was of her 15-year-old son because he called and asked her to come and get him from a party at an unsupervised home where drinking was taking place.

- We *embrace diversity* both in and outside our school walls. Example: The New City School has been participating in the annual St. Louis Pride Parade for 20 years, giving kids and families a chance to support the LGBTQ community.

- We continue showing *grit* in our quest to achieve a goal even if our friends and colleagues consider it wasted effort and have given up. Example: A teacher who wanted mindfulness incorporated in her school kept pushing against inertia by offering a free after-school mindfulness class for parents and students and getting time set aside for it at faculty meetings.

Teaching integrity to students can be challenging because we must encourage them to follow their conscience against authority while representing that very authority ourselves. Listening to students and empowering them is an important part of preparing them for the real world, yet it can result in a fine dance around rules and regulations. It's important to remind ourselves that developing students' integrity requires them at times to push against our authority.

Embracing Diversity

Respect for others goes beyond accepting or even appreciating others; to truly exhibit it, we must embrace those who are different than we are.

The demographics are clear: The United States is becoming more racially diverse each year. In 2018, *The New York Times* announced that "The foreign-born population in the United States has reached its highest share since 1910" (Tavernise, 2018), and the Brookings Institute predicts that whites in the United States will become a minority in 2045. But this effect will be seen and felt in our schools far before then: "Minorities will be the source of all of the growth in the nation's youth and working age population, most of the growth in its voters, and much of the growth in its consumers and tax base as far into the future as we can see" (Frey, 2018).

This increasing diversity, however, is not necessarily resulting in greater integration. According to the *U.S. News & World Report*, "a half century after the Fair Housing Act became a civil-rights landmark, multiple studies show housing in America is nearly as segregated as it was when LBJ enacted a law designed to eliminate it" (Williams, 2018). We should not be surprised that the vestiges of discrimination lie so close beneath the surface of our society; indeed, it is a fair question whether they are beneath the surface at all. Despite the inclusion of "life, liberty, and the pursuit of happiness" in the Declaration of Independence and the presence of the Statue of Liberty in New York Harbor, our country's history is littered with examples of injustice and oppression. This began with the genocide of Native Americans. As I noted in *The Formative Five* (Hoerr, 2017), 12 U.S. presidents owned black slaves. In *Between The World and Me*, Ta-Nehisi Coates (2015) says of black Americans, "Never forget that we were enslaved in this country longer than we have been free. Never forget that for 250 years black people were born into chains— whole generations followed by more generations who knew nothing but chains" (p. 70).

Recent events in the United States and around the world have illustrated the need to assert the importance of developing an awareness of and a sensitivity to diversity in students. Many of us were shaken by the events stemming from the 2017 "Unite the Right" Rally in Charlottesville, Virginia, in 2017, which culminated in the death of activist Heather Heyer. Similarly, the rancorous debates over Confederate monuments, the Black Lives Matter movement, and undocumented immigrants have exacerbated distrust and polarization. Permutations of these same issues echo across the oceans; regardless of how people vote or where they fall on the political continuum, people around the world agree that political discourse is at a terrible low.

At the same time, there is no doubt that there has been progress on the question of diversity. Fewer blatant signs of discrimination exist, LGBTQ relationships and marriages are commonplace in most areas (a *USA Today* poll says that 67 percent of Americans now support this [Madhani, 2018]), and there is a groundswell of support for those whose rights have often been ignored, such as through the disability rights and #MeToo movements. Yet our media are increasingly partisan, which allows people to engage only those perspectives that reinforce their beliefs. According to a 2018 Pew Research Center survey, "58 percent of U.S. adults say that having an increasing number of people of different races, ethnic groups and nationalities in the U.S. makes the country a better place to live" (Fingerhut, 2018). Verna Myers, a Cleveland attorney, captured how far we have come and yet how far we need to go when she told *The Cleveland Plain Dealer*, "Diversity is being invited to the party; inclusion is being asked to dance" (Cho, 2016).

In *The Formative Five*, I present the following steps to teaching students to embrace diversity: appreciating ourselves, recognizing others' diversities, appreciating others, planning, and implementing. These steps must be taken with intentionality and transparency; we need to be clear about our goals and our strategies and share them openly.

Grit

Grit came to public consciousness when Angela Duckworth's work on the concept was publicized by Paul Tough in the article "What If the Secret to Success Is Failure?" (2011) and book *How Children Succeed: Grit, Curiosity, and the Hidden Power of Character* (2012). My ASCD book *Fostering Grit* (2013) has garnered a great deal of attention, and even today, it seems like every article or book on leadership refers to the importance of grit.

Successful people come in many sizes and colors, degrees of talent and academic preparation, but the one thing they all possess is grit. That might not be the term they use; they might refer to their tenacity or perseverance, or talk about their passion and relentlessness, but it's grit all the same. "Grit is something I think young people need to grow toward," says Duckworth. "By definition, grit is passion for something that takes a long time to complete and perseverance" (Barshay, 2019).

In "We're Raising A Generation of Wimpy Kids" (2017) Amy Morin says, "many parents are becoming more like personal assistants to their children," and in 2019 we were shocked by the news that some parents paid bribes or had test scores falsified in order to gain their children's admission to college (Levenson & Morales, 2019).

The exasperation with ensuring that everyone succeeds is echoed by Betty Berdan, a high school junior, in her 2016 *New York Times* op-ed "Participation Trophies Send a Dangerous Message." "Trophies used to be awarded only to winners," she writes, "but are now little more than party favors: reminders of an experience, not tokens of true achievement. When awards are handed out like candy to every child who participates, they diminish in value." I hear this, too. When I give presentations, teachers and principals invariably decry their students' lack of grit. Educators with a couple of decades of experience talk about how this is more of a problem today than in the past. In our desire to help students succeed, we have provided an imbalance of positive reinforcement.

In *Where You Go Is Not Who You'll Be* (2015), a book that shows how the perceived quality of a college does not determine one's success, Frank Bruni writes: "Life is defined by little snags and big setbacks; success is determined by the ability to distinguish between the two and rebound from either." Perhaps Leila Janah put it best when she told the *New York Times,* "The biggest reason for success in entrepreneurship is not brilliance. It's not creative genius. It's the simple ability to not quit when things are really bad" (Bryant, 2017).

When interacting with someone who is highly skilled, it can be difficult to recognize the role that grit has played because their success appears so effortless. This happens to me when I watch the Olympics and consider the grace of a gymnast. "How talented and athletic they are," I think, "I could never do that." Well, first, I could never do that, and they *are* talented and athletic. However, my analysis fails to consider the thousands and thousands of hours of preparation and practice that this level of skill requires. Simone Biles, considered the greatest Olympic gymnast of all time, trains 32 hours per week. Olympic gold-medal swimmer Michael Phelps (23 gold, 38 medals overall) swims six hours per day, six days per week. NBA superstar shooter Steph Curry shoots 300 times during each practice in the season, and 500 shots per day during the off-season. Those hundreds of shots mean hundreds of misses, even for Steph Curry. This kind of intense regime—a manifestation of grit—is standard practice for athletes at all levels, as it is for high achievers in most other fields: Prior to being elected president in 1860, Abraham Lincoln had been defeated in four elections (one for the House, one for vice-president, and two for the Senate).

Too Much of a Good Thing?

Though educators have an obligation to teach success skills, they must also be cognizant of the downsides to pursuing each of the Formative Five too intently or without reflection.

The Downside of Empathy

Empathy is an emotional response to a person and situation. As wonderful and powerful as that can be—I've made the case that we need more empathy in the world—it may not be logical. In his book *Against Empathy: The Case for Rational Compassion* (2016), Paul Bloom writes:

———

Empathy has is merits. It can be a great source of pleasure, involved in art and fiction and sports, and it can be a valuable aspect of intimate relationships. And it can sometimes spark us to do good. But on the whole, it's a poor moral guide. It grounds foolish judgments and often motivates indifference and cruelty. It can lead to irrational and unfair political decisions, it can corrode certain important relationships, such as between a doctor and patient, and make us worse at being friends, parents, husbands, and wives. (pp. 2–3)

Another consideration is that too much empathy can result in a personal cost. People who are too empathic can have difficulty adhering to emotional boundaries. They may be unable to feel with others without losing their own balance; they can become so emotionally connected to others' plights that it results in excessive pain or inaction. In other words, an excess of empathy can be counterproductive and result in diminished actions to support others. The term *empathy fatigue* is used to describe what can happen when someone cares too deeply, too often, or about too many.

Teachers and principals who work with students with significant needs or who are undergoing severe trauma must take care not to develop empathy fatigue. Being an educator requires us to be understanding and caring, but we need to recognize that we have limits. The school year is a marathon, not a sprint, and we need to consciously allocate enough time for family, friends, and ourselves so that we can be fresh in May, end the year on a high note, and be enthusiastic about getting ready for the next school year.

The Downside of Self-Control

A certain amount of self-control is necessary in almost every situation, but an overreliance on it can result in rigidity, a lack of spontaneity, and an absence of enjoyment. Rather than assuming that self-control is always good and needed regardless of the situation, we need to step back and analyze its relative value. We should ask, "Where is self-control needed and how much is necessary?" Of course, we must also teach our students to do this. It's important, for example, to identify those situations in which self-control can inhibit problem solving. Successful brainstorming taps into the interplay and unique perspectives that can surface during group efforts, so excessive self-control in such a situation can be a roadblock. Those who credit too much of their success to self-control also risk projecting their ascetic mindset onto others by being overly impatient, critical, and condescending of those they perceive as lacking inner strength.

The Downside of Integrity

It may be difficult to envision too much integrity as being a negative, but we need to consider the context. There are some occasions when more progress can be made by standing back or remaining silent. Sometimes it is better—more strategic—to wait, either to assert ourselves at a more propitious time or to hang back so that others can take the lead. Being silent so that others will step forward is a conscious tactic that is held by every effective leader.

The Downside of Embracing Diversity

In her article "Has Diversity Lost Its Meaning?", Anna Holmes writes that diversity "has become both euphemism and cliché, convenient shorthand that gestures at inclusivity and representation without taking them seriously" (2015, p. 22). A "heroes and holidays" approach, where a handful of historical figures are singled out for praise, advances a superficial understanding of what it means to embrace diversity. While Black History Month was long overdue, it has given some schools license to ignore black history the other 11 months of the year.

The Downside of Grit

Too much grit can be used negatively or for ill purpose. The world would be better if miscreants had less grit! *Smart grit* means having both perseverance and the wisdom to know when it's time to quit. Not all problems can be solved, and some problems aren't worth the grit that is required to solve them. Grit also requires us to narrow our focus to a specific challenge, and too much tunnel vision can be a problem.

Advocating grit is sometimes seen as failing to appreciate the challenges that children may have due to their background and discrimination, but that is not accurate. For example, in "Grit Is in Our DNA" (*Education Week*, February 13, 2019) Bettina L. Love states, "Teachers and school leaders need to abandon teaching students to embrace 'grit'" and "these quick fixes pathologize African-Americans and are inherently anti-black" (p. 32). She accurately delineates the injustices, bondage, and trauma that African-Americans have experienced in the United States and how they have used grit to survive, ending with "We need teachers, school leaders, and policymakers who have grit for justice"; that is also true. Maintaining, however, that every child needs grit does not ignore or minimize previous and current discrimination and injustice. Rather, it affirms that every child needs grit, and reminds us that educators need grit to work for social justice.

* * *

In the next chapter, we will examine school culture, the expectations and norms that frame our perceptions and actions. Culture is powerful, but it can be changed and it can become a lever. We will see that culture can be a tool to support teaching the Formative Five.

3

What Is Culture?

Now in her seventh year of teaching at Pershing School, Stacey finds comfort in routine. She drives the same route to school and always parks in the same space. Carrying her laptop briefcase and a satchel filled with graded papers, a sandwich, and an apple, her mind is filled with what she has planned for the day as she walks through the school's front doors. She stops in the office to see if she has any messages, then walks down the main corridor, makes a right turn at the first corner, and enters her classroom. Her mind is roiling about the day ahead, and she gives little thought to her physical surroundings. Chances are that Stacey engages in a few greetings along the way to her class, but she doesn't give them any real attention. ("Hi, how are you?" is technically a question, but no one ever really expects an answer.) Students aren't due to arrive for 15 minutes, so now is the time to check e-mail and make last-minute preparations.

If you asked Stacey what messages she received between the time she entered the school and opened her classroom door, she might respond, "Messages? Not many. There was some mail from yesterday, mostly advertisements, and there were a dozen e-mails awaiting me, but that's it. Oh, and several people gave me a friendly greeting."

In fact, Stacey received many messages about her school's culture even though she may not have been conscious of them. What she saw, heard, and felt pointed to the school's values, student achievement, diversity, the roles of educators, and more. She felt expectations, rules, habits, and norms. Their omnipresence caused her to be unaware of them, just as a fish is likely unaware of water. Other than the personal greetings, these messages would be received by every adult or child who walked the halls and entered the office; they weren't targeted to Stacey. (And, in fact, virtually everyone would have been welcomed with the same friendly but superficial greeting that she received.) Those messages reflect the school's culture, even if it's unintentional.

Culture is "a kind of silent language," write Boris Groysberg and colleagues in their *Harvard Business Review* article "The Leader's Guide to Corporate Culture" (2018, p. 46). Although organizations are purportedly based on guidelines and procedures, people's feelings and actions are framed far more by the culture of their workplace than by written documents. "Culture is the tacit social order of an organization," continue Groysberg et al. "It shapes attitudes and behaviors in wide-ranging and durable ways. Culture norms define what is encouraged, discouraged, accepted, or rejected within a group" (p. 46).

The power of school culture is obvious if you visit two or more schools with the same grade range in the same school district. Although these schools operate under identical policies and guidelines, there is almost always a different feel between the schools. I see this firsthand when I visit schools to check in with the graduate students I teach in the University of Missouri–St. Louis' educational leadership program. Sometimes I visit schools that are only a 20-minute drive apart but seem to be in different countries or eras.

Culture is the impression we get from what we see, hear, feel, and taste; it is the salmagundi of values, expectations, habits, and norms that frame perceptions, form attitudes, and determine behavior. The culture that embraces Stacey as she enters Pershing School each day affects all aspects of the school's operation. It determines how faculty and committee meetings, parent-teacher conferences, and professional development activities are conducted and perceived. It frames how staff members view students and treat one another. Roland Barth (1990) says, "The school's culture dictates, in no uncertain terms, 'the way we do things around here.'" At 8:30 a.m., do the students quietly enter Stacey's classroom in an orderly fashion, or do they raucously spill into it, chatting and playing until she raises her voice to get their attention? Stacey's expectations for how students should enter her classroom each morning are framed by both the school's culture and the culture that she has established in her classroom.

Culture doesn't usually have a single author. Although an intense and strong-minded individual can have inordinate influence on a school's culture (whether he or she is an administrator or not), we typically give most weight to the thoughts and practices of our peers as a group. In most situations, our colleagues' expectations and perceptions have a greater influence on us than do formal policies or guidelines. That's true for Stacey and for everyone reading this paragraph.

The power of a school's culture is obvious in professional development sessions and at faculty meetings. Indeed, faculty meetings often are a Rosetta Stone for understanding a school's culture. If you observe a faculty meeting, you can tell a lot about a school's focus, tone, view of student achievement, and the relationships among each of the staff members.

Everyone Owns the Culture

Without a doubt, administrators have a powerful influence on a school's culture. Those of us who have worked in the same school with different principals have seen how perceptions and behaviors can change due to a leadership transition and different leaders. But the principal is not alone in possessing the ability to frame culture. Teachers have an opportunity to be an equal force in framing a culture to determine what is valued and how students are viewed.

Traditional management theory holds that organizations have a hierarchy and that a person's power—ability to influence others—can be determined by the position held within that hierarchy. Central office administrators have more power than principals who have more influence than teachers, and this clout enables people to frame culture. That's a simple idea and has some validity, but it doesn't fully capture the reality of what really happens in schools. Some roles have far more or less power than we might assume from looking at an organizational chart, and the range of power within a position can vary significantly by individual.

Imagine what would happen if all the adults working in your school were asked to identify two or three people whose opinions matter to them the most in the school. While some people would name the building principal, quite a few folks would identify others, perhaps a teammate or a teacher whose stellar reputation and arched eyebrows convey lots of power. In every school in which I worked, there were two or three teachers to whom others turned, formally and informally, for guidance, and there were also always a few teachers no one wanted to cross (including me!). The power held by these influencers would not show up on an organizational chart, but it enabled them to be instrumental in determining their school's culture.

The differences between the levels of power shown on an organizational chart and real-world patterns of influence became clear to me years ago when I participated in a districtwide project, the Issues Seminars, in which educators from all levels of the hierarchy met weekly in role-homogenous groups to discuss desegregation and began by talking about the obstacles that were making it more difficult for them to do their jobs. Groups of about 20 people were composed of central office administrators, secondary principals, secondary teachers, elementary principals, and elementary teachers. The discussions were spirited, random, and candid—minutes of each group's discussion were shared with other groups, but no individual comments or attributions were recorded. Unsurprisingly, everyone could identify an obstacle or two, and sometimes more. Students were underachieving, and people in every group felt constrained by a lack of power. The central office administrators felt limited by the local board of education and state legislature, but they saw these as challenges to overcome. Teachers said that principals were in charge, but they knew how to get what they needed. Neither the central office administrators nor the teachers saw their situations as debilitating, but this was not the case for the principals: Both elementary and secondary principals felt that they could not accomplish their jobs due in large part to the power held by both those "above" and "below" them on the organizational chart (i.e., the central office administrators and teachers). More than once, a principal said, "My teachers have more power than I do."

Perception is reality, so regardless of the formal power outlined in their job descriptions, the principals felt that they were hamstrung and acted accordingly. This is in contrast with what most organizational theorists would suggest. (The project took place years ago, but my many conversations with current principals suggest that things haven't changed all that much. In fact, e-mail and social media make it possible for just about anyone to communicate readily and publicly, and that has further served to constrain how administrators perceive their power.)

We would anticipate principals' sense of efficacy being somewhat constrained by their supervisors, but what accounts for them feeling that teachers also inhibited their actions? It's simple: A school's culture is incredibly powerful. In expressing that they didn't feel that they had enough organizational power to do their job well, the principals were responding to the fact that in their schools (indeed, in most schools), teachers have a significant role in creating and affirming the culture. Principals can issue edicts and directives, but many teachers' attitudes and behaviors are framed by other teachers, by the school's culture. A teacher-driven school culture can be so strong that principals become frustrated because they cannot elicit the behaviors that they want. Of course, a culture can also be strong and commensurate with the principal's thinking in a way that causes a synergy in which all perform to their ability and students benefit. Every principal I know talks about the strength of the faculty's mindset. If teachers are ready to pursue an issue and are open to learning, just about anything is possible. If, however, teachers are hesitant or oppositional—often with good reason, it must be noted—then progress will be halting at best.

It is vital for principals to appreciate that leadership is a shared responsibility; every faculty member should feel engaged and have a voice. When a failure to coordinate and lack of responsiveness occurs, it is likely because the principal has tried to lead by issuing edicts and directives instead of creating a culture that is built on relationships and trust. Teachers are going to own a lot of the culture in every school; strong principals widen the definition of leadership to ensure that all voices are heard and that everyone is engaged. That does not mean that everyone's vote is equal or that administrators abdicate their responsibilities; it does mean that everyone owns the culture.

Please take a minute here and think of the two or three factors that make it difficult for you to accomplish your job, regardless of your role. Consider how many of these obstacles could be mitigated by collaborating with others, either through the work of an ad hoc group of teachers or by a faculty committee. Regardless of the merit of our ideas or the strength of our efforts, trying to overcome problems alone is likely a Sisyphean task.

The Components of School Culture

"Culture is a carrier of meaning," writes Michael D. Watkins (2013). "Cultures provide not only a shared view of 'what is' but also of 'why is.' . . . culture is about 'the story' in which people in the organization are embedded, and the values and rituals that reinforce that narrative. It also focuses attention on the importance of symbols and the need to understand them—including the idiosyncratic languages used in organizations—in order to understand culture."

John Coleman's (2013) model of culture helpfully points out the often subtle cultural factors that determine our perceptions and behaviors, as shown in Figure 3.1. He posits the following factors as coming together to form culture: *vision, values, practices, people, narrative,* and *place.* Figure 3.2 reexamines the opening vignette in this chapter through the lens of Coleman's components of culture.

Unfortunately, most educators tend not to reflect on their school's culture. Either they simply aren't aware of its impact or they assume that there's not much they can do to change it. Their perceived lack of agency and ownership then causes them to not give it much attention. As we

FIGURE 3.1 **Coleman's Components of Culture (2013)**	
Component	**Explanation**
1. Vision	"A great culture starts with a vision or mission statement. These simple turns of phrase guide a company's values and provide it with purpose."
2. Values	"A company's values are the core of its culture. While a vision articulates a company's purpose, values offer a set of guidelines on the behaviors and mindsets needed to achieve that vision."
3. Practices	"Values are of little importance unless they are enshrined in a company's practices."
4. People	"No company can build a coherent culture without people who either share its core values or possess the willingness and ability to embrace those values."
5. Narrative	"Any organization has a unique history—a unique story. And the ability to unearth that history and craft it into a narrative is a core element of culture creation."
6. Place	"Place—whether geography, architecture, or aesthetic design—impacts the values and behaviors of people in a workplace."

will see, that's a mistake. An effective leader, regardless of title, recognizes the role of culture and works to influence it.

I often see a failure to appreciate school culture in the school interviews that are part of the graduate class on school culture that I teach at the University of Missouri–St. Louis. In preparing students to become principals, I assign a task at the beginning of the semester that requires them to interview a couple of teachers and an administrator at their school and ask them to describe its culture. The teachers and administrators are interviewed separately.

Three themes typically emerge from these interviews. First, regardless of whether they view the culture as positive or negative, teachers and administrators define culture by describing how people relate and communicate with one another, and there usually is a difference in the

FIGURE 3.2
Entering the School

Culture Component	Artifact/Touchstone
1. Vision/Mission	• Is the school's mission obvious? • Is it visibly posted in more than one place? • Are examples of achievement displayed?
2. Values	• Is it clear that the success and well-being of students is a goal? • Do walls and halls reflect a welcoming environment? • Are comfortable gathering spaces available? • Is security obvious yet appropriately subtle?
3. Practices	• What are the norms? • Is there a sign-in sheet? • Is everyone routinely welcomed in a friendly way?
4. People	• Do the adults display both care and commitment? • What kinds of greeting are offered by others? • What sort of interactions happen with students?
5. Narrative	• What rituals exist? • What morning greetings/habits are shared by all? • Do colleagues regularly connect to offer support and encouragement?
6. Place	• What formal signage exists? • Do walls and halls celebrate student success? • Do walls and halls celebrate student progress?

salience and priority of those relationships. Teachers chiefly talk about their relationships with peers and administrators as the primary factors in a school's culture, whereas administrators tend to talk about the relationships between teachers and students. Rarely do teachers or administrators mention their school's mission, physical environment, history, professional development offerings, or hiring and supervisory practices. Although there is merit in having the latest technology and we all want to work in a comfortable and safe setting, it's clear that our personal interactions affect much of what we see and do. Of course, those interactions are framed by and create the school's culture.

Second, when the people being interviewed describe why certain behaviors or activities take place (e.g., how students are treated or how faculty meetings are conducted), a common response of teachers *and* administrators is "That's just the way we do things here." People tend not to question the root causes of attitudes and behaviors. In fact, just as Stacey failed to notice many of the sights and sounds around her as she walked to her classroom, these kinds of responses reflect a lack of awareness of the many factors that determine culture.

Finally, the interview responses reveal a distinct difference between how teachers and administrators perceive their school's culture. Administrators tend to have a significantly more positive view of it than do the teachers—so much so that sometimes it sounds like they work at entirely different places. Rarely do teachers view their school's culture more positively than their administrators. Because they have different roles and responsibilities, at some level, teachers and administrators *should* view the world and their school's culture a bit differently; that is not a negative. Yet when it comes to large issues like student discipline, the role of standardized tests, school morale, and teacher engagement, the lack of similar perceptions and assessments indicates a real problem. After all, how can teachers and administrators successfully work to solve a problem if they do not agree on the nature of the problem (or if there even *is* a problem)? How can teachers stay enthusiastic and engaged if they feel that their input isn't valued, and how can administrators work to change that perception if they are unaware of it? Although different experiences and perspectives can be brought together to forge better solutions, this can only happen if the school's culture supports respect, candor, and an exchange of ideas.

Setting the Culture

In successful schools, teachers and administrators build the school culture together. Rather than vitiate either role, this approach capitalizes on everyone's creativity, investment, and energy. As Ken Robinson (2006) says, "The role of a creative leader is not to have all of the ideas; it's to create a culture where everyone can have ideas and feel that they're valued." In her TED Talk "Forget the Pecking Order at Work," Margaret Heffernan (2015) says:

> We've thought that success is achieved by picking the superstars, the brightest men, or occasionally women, in the room, and giving them all the resources and all the power. And the result has been . . . dysfunction and waste. If the only way the most productive can be successful is by suppressing the productivity of the rest, then we badly need to find a better way to work and a richer way to live.

In her talk, Heffernan quotes a musician who says, "It's the outstanding collaborators who enjoy the long careers, because bringing out the best in others is how they found the best in themselves." My philosophy of leadership is reflected in Heffernan's conclusion to her talk: "It is only when we accept that everybody has value that we will liberate the energy and imagination and momentum we need to create the best beyond measure."

Culture serves as a sort of shorthand for communicating and sharing knowledge. "A lot of knowledge in any kind of an organization is what we call task knowledge," says Howard Gardner. "These are things that people who have been there a long time understand are important, but they may not know how to talk about them. It's often called the culture of the organization" (Koch, 1996). Passing knowledge in these formal and informal ways, with and without language, is endemic to humans. In *She Has Her Mother's Laugh* (2018), Carl Zimmer describes how groups of children improved their problem-solving skills by watching other children solve similar problems: "Many anthropologists now argue that this so-called cumulative culture is a hallmark of our species" (p. 460).

In the next five chapters, we will use culture as a tool to develop students' Formative Five success skills. Coleman's model offers six separate culture components, but I have merged the first two: vision/mission and values. To the degree that culture is developed by teachers and administrators, working together, everyone will benefit.

Vision, Mission, Values Survey

Before reading this chapter, please take a few minutes and respond to these survey items. An explanation and scoring system appear at the end of this survey.

Please indicate your perceptions by circling SA (strongly agree), A (agree), D (disagree), or SD (strongly disagree) by each item.

1. Our school's mission statement is reviewed annually.

    SA   A   D   SD

2. A mission statement should focus on academic and intellectual development.

    SA   A   D   SD

3. Volunteer or service learning programs should only be pursued if they stem from the mission statement.

    SA   A   D   SD

4. A mission statement should be created by administrators and approved by the board of a school.

    SA   A   D   SD

5. A school should have its own mission statement.

   SA   A   D   SD

6. Values and mission have little impact on teaching.

   SA   A   D   SD

7. Values can and should be taught as part of any subject-matter curriculum.

   SD   D   A   SA

8. Analyzing a mission statement by determining which words are addressed in a school's practice can be a powerful faculty activity.

   SA   A   D   SD

9. Social action activities can be good if they do not detract from academic time.

   SA   A   D   SD

10. The values stated in a mission statement should be oriented to achievement and employment.

    SA   A   D   SD

11. The values stated in a mission statement should be oriented to achievement, job preparation, and emotional development.

    SA   A   D   SD

12. Sometimes a difficult incident can lead to a positive reflection on values.

    SA   A   D   SD

13. Understanding the distinction between honesty and integrity is not appropriate for elementary-age students.

    SA   A   D   SD

14. Service learning activities can help students reflect on their values.

SA   A   D   SD

15. The beneficiaries of a social action activity are those who produce the efforts as well as those who receive them.

SA   A   D   SD

The culture component surveys are designed to facilitate reflection and dialogue. After you have determined your score, I suggest that you answer the questions under item 1 below. Then, after two or three colleagues have also completed the survey, compare responses using the questions under item 2.

1. Does this score capture what happens in your school? Are there issues not addressed that you think are significant? Would your colleagues agree with your responses? If not, why might that be? Would your responses surprise colleagues?

2. On what items do you and your colleagues agree? When you disagree, why is that? Is there a correlation between how you see things and your position, years of experience, or another demographic factor? Were you previously aware of these different perceptions?

Scoring:

1. For items 1, 5, 7, 8, 11, 12, 14, and 15, give yourself 4 points for each SA and 3 points for each A. Subtract 4 points for each SD and 3 points for each D. Subtotal A= _____

2. For items 2, 3, 4, 6, 9, 10, and 13, give yourself 4 points for each SD and 3 points for each D. Subtract 4 points for each SA and 3 points for each A. Subtotal B= _____

3. Grand total (A + B) = _____

What Your Score Means:

- If your score is less than 30, your school needs to radically change how values are framed to support the vision, mission, and values component.
- If your score is between 30–39, your school should review practices to see where improvements can be made in the vision, mission, and values component.
- If your score is between 40–49, your school is doing a good job of supporting the vision, mission, and values component, and you should look to see which area(s) need more attention.
- If your score is more than 50, your school is doing an excellent job of supporting the vision, mission, and values component.

4

Vision, Mission, Values

I suspect that most of your colleagues don't know your school's vision or mission statement. The values that they esteem are almost a given; everyone wants students to learn 21st century skills, succeed academically, and be good citizens, but that's about it. The vision and mission may be prominently posted, and possibly included on stationery, but chances are that they are not referred to during professional development sessions or in meetings with parents. Consequently, too often these goals remain aphorisms that sound good but mean little. That's because a tighter definition of vision and mission may lead to contention. Everyone wants world peace but deciding where boundaries should be drawn and how resources should be allocated quickly gets contentious. The desire to avoid disputes is evident in the mission statements of many schools and school districts, as shown in Figure 4.1. Many worthy goals and outcomes are mentioned in these mission statements, but how informative are they, really? To what degree would any of them frame your behaviors? This is not to suggest anything negative about the quality of these schools. It's understood that mission statements represent our highest hopes and most ambitious goals.

FIGURE 4.1

School Mission Statements

School	Mission Statement
Overbrook High School	Overbrook High School is dedicated to providing academic programs and opportunities for every child to develop their individual talents and abilities in order to be prepared for college and careers in the 21st century.
Weston Public Schools	To educate, equip, and inspire all students to achieve their full potential and enrich their communities.
Washington Middle School	Washington Middle School is a positive and supportive student-centered learning environment. We want our students to have fun, love learning, achieve their individual potential, and care about each other. Therefore, we emphasize enthusiasm for learning, respect for others, and responsibility for our actions. At Washington, we strive to provide a safe, orderly, and respectful environment where students experience academic success through challenging, diverse, and engaging learning experiences.
Adrian Wilcox High	The purpose of Wilcox High School is to educate, empower, and enable all students to become caring, contributing citizens who can succeed in an ever-changing world. Wilcox High School is committed to focusing on high expectations and individual academic success and to creating a community of respect and responsibility.
Lakeside School	The mission of Lakeside School is to develop in intellectually capable young people the creative minds, healthy bodies, and ethical spirits needed to contribute wisdom, compassion and leadership to a global society. We provide a rigorous, academic program through which effective educators lead students to take responsibility for learning. We are committed to sustaining a school in which individuals representing diverse cultures and experiences instruct one another in the meaning and value of community and in the joy and importance of lifelong learning.
Travis B. Bryan High	The Bryan High School community is committed to developing successful, life-long learners who think, care, and serve in a global society.

Ronald Reagan High School	The International Baccalaureate aims to develop inquiring, knowledgeable, and caring young people who help to create a better and more peaceful world through intercultural understanding and respect. To this end the organization works with schools to develop challenging programs of international education and rigorous assessment. These programs encourage students across the world to become active, compassionate and lifelong learners who understand that other people, with their differences, can also be right.
Fridley Public Schools	As a world class community of learners, Fridley Public Schools aims to develop internationally minded students. We challenge ourselves, our students, and our community to become caring and knowledgeable life-long learners who inquire and take action to create a better world.

"A lot is asked of missions statements," writes Terry Heick in "The Problem with Most School Mission Statements" (2018). "They have to sell the school, please the superintendent, and rally the community. Only they read like inscriptions on national monuments, or the elegies of fallen heroes." Academics, skills, or learning are mentioned in each of the statements in Figure 4.1, and that's appropriate, but the lack of differentiation is obvious, and it raises the question of what actual differences we might see among these schools beyond size, location, demographics, and wealth. Based on their mission statements, how might the schools' curriculum, pedagogy, or assessment differ? The mission statement for Lakeside High mentions "diverse cultures and experiences" and the one for Ronald Reagan High refers to "learners who understand that other people, with their differences, can also be right," but those are the only explicit references to our country's changing population and the pressing need to understand and appreciate one another. Social-emotional learning is alluded to in half the statements, but not in any specific way, calling into question how much each school really focuses on it.

Mission Statements and Performance vs. Moral Character

Educators should use the Lickona and Davidson model of performance versus moral character (see p. 7 in Chapter 1) to determine the relative influence of SEL-related language in their school's mission statements. As a reminder, performance character qualities are those oriented to success in the world of work (grit, self-control, work ethic, ingenuity), whereas moral character qualities are those focused on success in relationships (caring, respect, justice). Often a school's mission is more oriented to performance character attributes because the focus is on preparing students for employment and higher education. In reviewing the character qualities of the schools listed in Figure 4.1, for example, we see a strong disparity between the two areas, with much more focus given to performance character:

- **Performance character terms:** Academic programs, individual talents and abilities, student-centered, achieve potential, enthusiasm for learning, academic success, wisdom, leadership, learning, lifelong learning, life-long learners, inquiring, knowledgeable
- **Moral character terms:** Respect, responsibility, caring, contributing, ethical, and compassion

Performance character terms are appropriate and necessary, but this kind of disparity creates an imbalance in students' SEL skill set. Because we want a world in which people show respect, are caring, and behave responsibly, schools should more often explicitly identify moral character attributes as ones that they value and want to pursue.

The power of moral character can be seen when we analyze what we do to help kids enjoy learning and become better people. One of my favorite faculty meetings is the one I began by referring to the fact that *joyful learning* was in our school's mission statement and asking teachers to share examples of it from their classrooms. The ensuing discussion generated a remarkable amount of dialogue and laughter—so much so that I had trouble regaining the group's attention! The question had not only reinforced an important aspect of our mission but also led to faculty members sharing becoming a part of the school's narrative. I am sure that many teachers shared what they said and heard at the dinner table that evening and later in the week with colleagues.

Examples in Action

Below are some examples of schools that have taken a proactive approach to ensuring that SEL and the Formative Five skills are meaningfully addressed both in their mission and in practice.

Ella Baker Elementary School

When principal Kim Bilanko helped to set up Ella Baker Elementary School in Redmond, Washington—a school centered on the Formative Five skills plus curiosity, optimism, and gratitude (as identified by Paul Tough)—she started with the expectation that "the mission, vision, and values we hold would become our driving force, our mindset, in all decisions that we make." She continues:

Each person who was hired to our team was asked to watch Simon Sinek discuss the importance of determining the *why* of an organization. Then they were asked to evaluate their own purpose by thinking about why they are a teacher. I asked them to free write their thoughts—with no rules. They could jot, draw, journal, or list ideas. After they were done, they were asked to bring key words and phrases to our planning meeting. They sat in partners and small groups and shared their why. This was an incredible moment, watching everyone sharing their passion for education simultaneously. The open-ended task led to creativity, passion, and deep emotion. One teacher wrote a beautiful song that had us all in tears. . . .

We are striving to create environments that promote and develop student's moral and performance character. We do this by integrating SEL in everything. If we are starting a new club, or if our PTSA is planning a new event, we align it with our mission, vision, and values. Whether it is professional development or a decision around a procedure, we are constantly revisiting our document to ensure we make decisions that align with our collective values. This helps us keep focused on the right work.

It's important to share the mission and educate everyone about what this means. "The physical environment of a school sends a message to students, staff, and families," Bilanko says. "For us, the walls speak volumes about who we are. We want to ensure our environment is aligned with our mission, vision, and values. Since character building is an essential aspect of our school, our eight character traits are found everywhere in our hallways. We value students and families feeling connected to our school."

El Paso Leadership Academy

Omar Yanar, CEO of the El Paso Leadership Academy, takes the same approach as Bilanko. Each summer, faculty at the Academy take part in the Summer of Academic Revolution (SOAR), a week-and-a-half long professional development activity. "This time is designed for teachers to reflect on our mission and our core values," says Yanar. "It's an interactive time, and they work collaboratively to develop lessons and activities that focus on college preparation and community engagement. Throughout, we consistently *over*-communicate our core values." The Academy uses the acronym CRSHH (pronounced "crush") to indicate its core values of collaboration, responsibility, smart, hungry, and humble. They use this term in their assemblies, and Yanar encourages staff members to include it in communications to students and parents.

Fairway School

Brittney Dailey, a 3rd grade teacher at Fairway School in the Rockwood (Missouri) School District, led a service-learning project, "Spread the Love," to help children who were undergoing cancer treatments. Her students created presentations for other classes, including one on how their efforts were tied to the idea of empathy. Dailey and her class used the term *empathy* often throughout the project. This Rockwood School District mission statement reads, "We do whatever it takes to ensure all students realize their potential," and Dailey's class worked to make that happen even for children who were receiving treatments for a life-threatening illness.

Arundel High School

A highlight at Arundel High School in Gambrills, Maryland, is the Global Community Citizenship Class, a course that focuses on SEL and the Formative Five. In the *Capital Gazette* (2018), Lauren Lumpkin writes that the impetus for the course was a racist petition some students had distributed. Rather than simply reprimanding the students, the faculty responded by developing a 9th grade course that addressed racism and bias head-on:

Students begin the Global Community Citizenship Class with lessons on self-exploration and discovery. Personality tests are given for homework; community circles that engage students and teachers in an open discussion are classroom mainstays. 'We learned about ourselves, our personality traits, where we came from,' said sophomore Elliana Anderson. 'We started to think about what factors into what shaped the people around us.' The semester-long class also includes lessons on cultural competency, tolerance, stereotypes, biases and empathy, teachers said. Students said they have learned how to communicate more effectively with people they disagree with, something they say is missing from public discourse.

"The class focuses on building relationships, teaching kids to be active listeners—to give body attention, to restate, and to use the other person's name in doing so," Johanna Ricker, the program's team leader, tells Lumpkin. "It is a space of integrity, where we value students as human and help them learn about themselves and how to make a positive difference in the world." Ricker shared how she had recently focused on integrity by beginning a class with the question "Which value do you wish that every human had in common?" Students then walked in two parallel circles while music played in the background; when the music stopped, they stopped, turned to the person next to them, gave a high-five, and shared the value they had identified. (Respect, honesty, love, kindness, and integrity were often cited.) "If we all truly acted with integrity, the world would be so much better," she told the class. The class also regularly discusses ethical dilemmas (e.g., "Is it acceptable to rob a store to get food for a person who is starving? Does it matter if the store's loss will be covered by insurance?") to get students to consider *why* they feel the way they do.

The Global Community Citizenship Class aligns well with Arundel High School's mission to "strengthen collaboration between our school, families and community, create a safe and supportive environment, and challenge students to become lifelong learners and productive, responsible citizens." Clearly the program is successful, because the school district's governing board made it a graduation requirement for all Anne Arundel County students beginning in 2019.

North Glendale Elementary School

As a first-year principal at North Glendale Elementary School in Glendale, Missouri, Masa Massenburg-Johnson decided to lead her faculty in creating the school's mission statement. The district's mission statement was good, but she thought this experience would help draw her faculty together into a team, especially because she was replacing a long-standing principal. "We were in transition, and I believed that this process would allow them to grieve, heal, and accept change," she says. The faculty formed vertical teams of representatives from various grades and met approximately twice per month. After working for almost a school year, they produced the following three potential school mission statements, ensuring that they aligned to the district's mission:

1. We are passionate, resilient, empathic, connected, relationship-builders. We are North Glendale. We are one.

2. We will approach life and learning with perseverance, flexibility, and empathy.
3. We are all lifelong learners. We are all compassionate teachers. We are all together.

Staff voted on the statement that best reflected the school's mission and settled on number three: *We are all lifelong learners. We are all compassionate teachers. We are all together.* The faculty will use professional development sessions during the following year to design strategies for putting this statement into action.

New City School

Engaging students in service-learning activities can be an effective way to teach empathy. Jessica Brod Millner, chair of the Social Action Committee at New City School in St. Louis, Missouri, says that the goal of their school "is for children to know 'Why am I doing this? What am I learning through this experience, about myself and the world in which I live?'" To be successful, she says, projects should be engaging, raise an awareness of others' perspectives, and make a difference in the lives of the volunteers and the people in need:

_____

We participate in a range of activities, including collecting food to support families in need, sorting and organizing at a food pantry, cleaning the neighborhood park, and planting vegetables in a community garden. Empathy is emphasized in every activity. We talk about doing more than providing or helping, but also trying to imagine how other people feel. Students are challenged to step into another person's shoes and to imagine how other individuals may feel while experiencing the same situation. As part of our efforts to go beyond thinking and feeling and move to action—something that comes from empathizing with others—we have scheduled weekend family field trips to organizations that could use our support and held gatherings, where we invite families to join us at school to do hands-on projects in small groups, such as creating fleece blankets for children in need, packaging backpacks of food for hungry children, drawing pictures and making crafts to be delivered to nursing homes or children's hospitals, writing letters to our military, cleaning up parks and neighborhoods, making lunches for people in need and delivering them to a shelter, to name just a few. We always talk about the importance of developing our students' empathy, understanding how others feel.

Empathy is a focus of Arthur Culbert, St. Louis' Urban Gardener (that's his official title). A volunteer, he leads New City School students in growing crops—corn, collard greens, sweet potatoes, and other organic vegetables and fruits—on a vacant lot and donating them to a food pantry. "The pantry provides the setting for empathy," says Culbert. "Students meet their new friends and learn that they do not have access to fresh vegetables and fruits because they cannot afford them and do not live close to a supermarket." The garden experience is part of the 4th grade's "Citizens Make a Difference" theme, the goal of which is for students to become involved in an altruistic cause as a result of their empathic feelings. Culbert notes that "students begin to realize what a gift it is, through service, to help grow, harvest, and deliver needed vegetables and fruits for others."

Mission Statements and Actions

In the educational leadership class that I teach, I have students attend a school board meeting and ask them to observe two things: (1) the degree to which the actions of the board pursue the goals noted in the district's mission statement, and (2) the degree to which the conduct of the board itself reflects the mission statement. The follow-up discussion in our class is always fascinating. Often, there's little evidence of the mission statement in the decisions of the board or their interactions despite the fact that the vision/mission statement is prominently displayed on signs and banners. (Notable exceptions can be when students receive awards or perform or when staff members' successes are acknowledged.)

Too often, this kind of disconnect also occurs in schools at faculty or committee meetings, during parent education evenings, and even

during professional development sessions. We have a vision and pro-
claim a mission, yet it's easy to get caught in the activity-response cycle:
We do things because they need to be done and have always been done,
without stepping back and asking how our actions help us achieve our
mission. Distractions and deterrents abound, so our vision and mission
should be our lodestar, something that ensures that our efforts are on
target and focused.

At Your School

- What's the vision?
- How widespread is it known?
- Does it determine people's behaviors?

Practices Survey

Before reading this chapter, please take a few minutes and respond to these survey items. An explanation and scoring system appear at the end of this survey.

Please indicate your perceptions by circling SA (strongly agree), A (agree), D (disagree), or SD (strongly disagree) by each item.

1. Our school recognizes and cites student effort, tenacity, and trajectory.

    SA   A   D   SD

2. Faculty meetings rarely focus on diversity and inclusion.

    SA   A   D   SD

3. We use assemblies, walls, and halls to recognize students and adults who are kind and care for others.

    SA   A   D   SD

4. Principles of restorative justice are used to help students reflect on how their behavior may have caused harm and what they can do to repair that harm.

    SA   A   D   SD

5. Honesty is the goal in student preparation.

    SA   A   D   SD

6. We take the time to consider each student's learning strengths and challenges, personal history, and home environment.

    SA   A   D   SD

7. We should never push students to become very frustrated.

    SA   A   D   SD

8. Posted signs that identify misbehaviors and delineate their consequences are common.

    SA   A   D   SD

9. Students of all demographic, socioeconomic status, and abilities see themselves on walls, in halls, and playing leadership roles.

    SA   A   D   SD

10. Adults are comfortable sharing their positions in faculty meetings and the teachers' lounge even if their views are in the minority.

    SA   A   D   SD

11. We intentionally teach students about the varying perspectives that people hold and what might cause these differences.

    SA   A   D   SD

12. Faculty meeting agendas are created by administrators.

    SA   A   D   SD

13. We should avoid students being uncomfortable with diversity.

SA   A   D   SD

14. Students set personal goals in many classes, and these are shared publicly or with faculty members.

SA   A   D   SD

15. Students who show little effort in school will not exhibit grit in nonscholastic settings.

SA   A   D   SD

The culture component surveys are designed to facilitate reflection and dialogue. After you have determined your score, I suggest that you answer the questions under item 1 below. Then, after two or three colleagues have also completed the survey, compare responses using the questions under item 2.

1. Does this score capture what happens in your school? Are there issues not addressed that you think are significant? Would your colleagues agree with your responses? If not, why might that be? Would your responses surprise colleagues?
2. On what items do you and your colleagues agree? When you disagree, why is that? Is there a correlation between how you see things and your position, years of experience, or another demographic factor? Were you previously aware of these different perceptions?

Scoring:

1. For items 1, 3, 4, 6, 9, 10, 11, and 14, give yourself 4 points for each SA and 3 points for each A. Subtract 4 points for each SD and 3 points for each D. Subtotal A= _____
2. For items 2, 5, 7, 8, 12, 13, and 15, give yourself 4 points for each SD and 3 points for each D. Subtract 4 points for each SA and 3 points for each A. Subtotal B= _____

3. Grand total (A + B) = _____

What Your Score Means:

- If your score is less than 30, your school needs to radically change how values are framed to support the practices component.
- If your score is between 30–39, your school should review practices to see where improvements can be made in the practices component.
- If your score is between 40–49, your school is doing a good job of supporting the practices component, and you should look to see which area(s) need more attention.
- If your score is more than 50, your school is doing an excellent job of supporting the practices component.

5

Practices

Our school practices must integrate SEL in each academic area, in all extracurricular activities, and in every location. Social-emotional learning should be part of the fiber of after-school activities, athletics, and assemblies. It should be evident on walls, in halls, and on signage. The Executive Summary of *From a Nation at Risk to a Nation at Hope*, the 2019 report from Aspen Institute's National Commission on Social, Emotional, and Academic Development, puts it well:

> Educating the whole student requires rethinking teaching and learning so that academics and students' social, emotional, and cognitive development are joined not just occasionally, but throughout the day. Students are intentionally taught these skills and asked to exercise them as they learn academic content and interact with peers and adults. Learning environments that support the whole student are physically and emotionally safe and are based on warm, supportive relationships—including those between children and teachers that are fundamental to learning. (p. 1)

Cultures can vary widely among schools in a district and even between grade levels or academic departments within the same school. Although everyone is pursuing the same vision and mission statements, the result can be quite different norms and practices. In "The Leader's Guide to Corporate Culture," Groysberg and colleagues (2018) state that "cultural norms define what is encouraged, discouraged, accepted, or rejected within a group" (p. 46). These norms are our practices, how we bring our school's vision, mission, and values to life. They stem from how we see the role of educators, the ways we interact with others (students, their parents, colleagues, and the community), and our approach to curriculum, pedagogy, grading, and professional development activities.

Faculty Meetings

The practices at faculty meetings serve as a Rosetta Stone of a school's culture. Just as translating the script on the stone led to the understanding of the Egyptian hieroglyphs that documented the anniversary of the coronation of Ptolemy V Epiphanes as King of Egypt in 196 BCE (I'll bet you didn't know that either!), analyzing the meetings—how often and where are they held? What is the agenda and who plays what roles?—yields telling insights.

How would you characterize your school's faculty meetings? Take a moment and fill out the chart in Figure 5.1.

Unfortunately, many faculty meetings are not engaging, productive, or insightful; a strong learning focus is not the norm. I know this because the title of an article I wrote, "What If Faculty Meetings Were Voluntary?" (2009b), always elicits smiles and eye rolls. Most people say they'd never go to a faculty meeting if they had that option. This is a lost opportunity. Faculty meetings should be designed so that they are relevant, interesting, and sometimes even fun, addressing academic topics, schoolwide issues, and students' and educators' SEL. When that happens, people will want to attend, which sets the stage for increased learning. A practice of vibrant and inclusive meetings would speak volumes about a school's culture and faculty engagement.

FIGURE 5.1

Faculty Meeting Focus Chart

Our faculty meetings . . .	Yes	No
1. Are scheduled at least monthly		
2. Are used for more than simply conveying information		
3. Have time allocated for gathering, congeniality		
4. Have food and snacks available		
5. Feature teachers playing significant roles		
6. Engage teachers in discussion		
7. Often include fun and laughter		
8. Begin and end on time		
9. Are very well attended		
10. Are well planned or organized		
11. Have time for responding to open-ended questions		
12. Are designed for sharing ideas and practices		
13. Occasionally feature an educator sharing strategies		
14. Occasionally feature a presentation by a guest		
15. Include celebration of staff successes		
16. Have clear agendas		
17. Have agendas to which all staff are asked to contribute		

Scoring and Implications: Add the number of yes responses. A score of 10–12 warrants a high-five; your faculty meetings are learning meetings, designed to offer support and facilitate growth. A score of 6–9 is promising, but more can be done to improve the tone and effectiveness of meetings. A score of 5 or less warrants a discussion about the purpose and design of faculty meetings.

The Smile Quotient

Schoolwide practices, common experiences throughout the building, can generate a special power. When I describe the qualities of a good school, I include a high "smile quotient." As I walk through a school, I want to see smiles on faces of kids and adults. Rather than indicating a casual attitude toward learning, lots of smiles mean that everyone is pleased to be at the school because they are engaged and succeeding.

To raise the smile quotient at my school, I initiated the "10-foot rule": Whenever adults came within 10 feet of another adult, they were to make eye contact and offer a friendly greeting. (The practice of adults offering a smile and greeting to any children they saw had already been established.) I figured that increasing the connections among adults would result in a greater comfort level that would lead to people taking the time and making the effort to know and understand one another. When I began promoting the 10-foot rule, my primary goal was to have parents connect with other parents, but it soon became clear that this practice would benefit our staff, too. As is the case in many schools, some of my teachers were so busy and preoccupied that they sometimes walked through the hall in a daze, acknowledging neither peers nor parents. In fact, their focus was a positive one because they were reflecting on their last lesson or planning their next class, but the negative effect remained. That changed after we instituted the 10-foot rule. More eye contact led to increased smiles, which resulted in more conversations and greater connections. This is a small practice that goes a long way toward creating culture that promotes SEL. (I later heard from a Texas A&M alum that the 10-foot rule was emphasized during his freshman orientation and was part of their campus tradition. Subsequently, I learned that Sam Walton also encouraged this practice among Walmart employees in his stores.)

A theme of this book is that when we implement SEL and develop the Formative Five, we cannot go from values/vision/mission to students, and leapfrog the adults. We need to develop SEL in our staff members, and we also must find opportunities to engage students' parents with SEL. School leaders, whatever their title, need to very visibly walk the SEL talk. That is because while formalized schoolwide issues are powerful, smaller interactions also have a significant effect.

Every Interaction Is an Opportunity

I recently read *Rocket Boys* (1998) by Homer H. Hickman Jr., the author's autobiographical account of growing up in Coalwood, West Virginia, as the son of a coal mine superintendent. Hickman became interested in science, particularly rockets, at an early age, and continually found ways to experiment with designs and fuels, much to the concern of his mother and frustration of his father. Miss Riley, a chemistry and physics teacher at Big Creek High School, took the time to know him and see his potential; she stood out for her support of and confidence in him. Because of her encouragement, Hickman entered the National Science Fair—and won! He ended up working for NASA and writing several books. While many people played important roles in his success, it was Miss Riley's interactions with Hickman—giving him a book about rocketry, for example—that changed his trajectory (pun intended).

The powerful role of a teacher is also highlighted in Tara Westover's remarkable memoir, *Educated* (2018). Westover earned her PhD despite not attending school before college, and in the book she lavishes her post-secondary writing teacher, Professor Steinberg at Cambridge University, with praise: "No comma, no period, no adjective or adverb was beneath his interest. He made no distinction between grammar and content, between form and substance" (p. 236). Clearly, Professor Steinberg knew and believed in Westover.

A few years ago, I attended the Affton (Missouri) School District's Foundation Hall of Fame dinner. This is an annual event designed to raise funds for students' college scholarships and for professional development grants that are awarded to some of the district's teachers. The focus of the grants ranged from developing curriculum to working with technology to identifying community resources that could be integrated in the school. It was very gratifying to see the teachers' visible excitement when their grant proposals were read and met with applause by the audience. The awards were followed by a dinner that included a performance by the Affton High School choir and words of pride from the principal and some local politicians.

The evening was an emotional high, filled with achievements and optimism. My favorite moment—and one that captures the power of simple practices—came near the end of the evening, when the Foundation honored six teachers who had been identified as having an extraordinarily positive influence on their students. The teachers were selected through a process of recommendations from former students of the school. To enthusiastic applause, these teachers were identified and called to the podium, where they stood a bit embarrassed while a wonderful story was told about each of them. After their story was shared, the teacher received a plaque, several hugs, and lots more applause. The teachers came from elementary, middle, and high schools, and while their curriculum focus and assignments varied, the stories told about them made it very clear what they had in common: They each brought high expectations, pedagogical expertise, and real care to their students.

But one teacher's recognition stands out in my mind and even brought tears to my eyes. When the name of Bob Brunette, a high school physical education teacher and football coach, was called, the audience roared in approval. Someone at my table said, "His teams are always good!" Another person added, "They kick butt!" I wondered if his teams' championships would be cited, and if any of his former players would speak.

"We heard quite a few wonderful things about the coach," said the evening's moderator after the applause had died down, "and it's clear that many of you know him, but one comment stood out, and I want to ask the person who made it to join us up here and share his thoughts."

A young man, probably in his late 20s, came to the microphone.

"You probably don't know me," he said. "I wasn't an athlete and wasn't very visible in high school, and I've been living out of town since I graduated. I went to California to pursue my music career and have been there ever since, but I nominated Coach Brunette and wanted to be here tonight."

He paused for a deep breath before continuing.

"I never even had Coach as one of my teachers. But he taught across from a room where I had a class, and Coach was always standing in the hall when classes passed. Just about every time I saw him, he asked,

'How's your music going?' Sometimes he would follow up to see if I had any gigs scheduled or would ask how a gig had gone. He remembered. Occasionally he would ask me about the music. He said hi to lots of people, and he took the time to know me. Maybe he did that for others, too. All I know is how I felt.

"Things weren't always good for me then, but I knew that Coach would ask and Coach would listen. And I wasn't even an athlete!" At this, he and the coach both smiled and faced one another. "I knew you cared, Coach, and in those days, I really needed that kind of care. I'm on a successful path now, and I know that I wouldn't be there today without your care back then. You took the time to know me, even though I wasn't one of your players or students, and it meant a lot. Thank you."

They hugged, the crowd applauded, and mine were not the only eyes that filled with tears.

I called Coach Brunette after this dinner despite never having met him and he cheerfully chatted with me. He told me that some of his former football players had recently visited him to surprise him with cake for his 90th birthday. He recalled the young man and the dinner, and he took great delight in talking about many other students that he remembered. He used to make a point of standing in the corner as classes were switching so that he could see and greet as many students as possible. He worked to learn their names.

The beauty of this story is that it illustrates the power of even our smallest practices. The coach changed someone's life not through his teaching or his coaching, but simply through his interactions in the hall. Coach Brunette deserves the credit, and it's important to note that the school's culture supported his interactions.

Intentionality, Transparency, and Collaboration

In all of our practices (indeed, in all of our interactions), we need to remember that we should act with intentionality, transparency, and an eye toward collaboration.

Intentionality means that we must deliberate and prioritize our practices. We should choose strategies as part of an overall quest, balancing time, energy, and resources. We also need to understand that some institutional and individual discomfort is a necessary cost of changing practices, and it will occur whenever we discard what we used to do or try something that is different. Counterintuitive as it might seem, if everyone is happy, that means we aren't being creative or aggressive enough. As Franklin Roosevelt once said, "Judge me by the enemies I have made."

Transparency means being public and clear about what our practices are, why we implement them, and what our hopes are for the future. We must explain the conditions or changes that cause us to act as we do, presenting information in various venues and ways to ensure that everyone understands. It is better for folks to hear the rationale and question it than for them to be unaware of our motivations and speculate. As Brené Brown says, "In the absence of data, we will always make up stories (2015, p. 79)."

Collaboration means creating opportunities for teachers and administrators to work together and develop practices, thus increasing the likelihood that they will be better designed. "Culturally proficient school leaders use effective collaborative and communication skills to engage nonformal leaders in ways that make sense of their knowledge and skills," write Lindsey, Robins, and Terrell in *Cultural Proficiency* (2009).

Leveraging a Lesson to Teach Multiple Success Skills

A new playground is being built adjacent to Grace-St. Luke's School, a preK–8 school in Memphis, Tennessee, that has embraced the Formative Five skills to support values-based education and focus on developing the whole child. Every classroom features a Formative Five poster—featuring, for example, a hand with each of the five fingers representing one of the success skills—and the school's halls are adorned with student-created work, art, and paragraphs that speak to the Formative Five. At the beginning of the year, all the teachers at the school reviewed the importance of the Formative Five skills among themselves and with parents during Back to School Night.

The school's two 4th grade teachers, Jane Williams and Juan Roncal, believed that asking their students for input regarding the design of the new playground was a wonderful way to teach the success skills. They began by emphasizing to students that their task was not to design a playground for their friends or for the 4th grade alone, but for all students in grades 3–8. To do this, the 4th grade students were told that they needed to put their desires for the new playground aside and figure out what other students want by using empathy (a term the teachers had discussed and often used with students).

The 4th graders were divided into teams of six (to increase the opportunities for students to lead and work together) and given their first task: to design a survey that could be sent to every student in grades 3–8. Creating the survey and trying to anticipate how children's needs might vary due to their age, interest, or bodily-kinesthetic talent helps the students to develop their empathy skills. Student-created survey questions ask respondents what they like to do at recess, whether they like the playground as currently designed, and how they would rank the importance of a range of items (e.g., monkey bars, an outdoor bathroom, a basketball court, a charging station).

Williams and Roncal also wanted to stress additional Formative Five success skills during this project:

- *Self-control:* Prior to dividing the students into teams, they engage students in a discussion about the qualities of good teamwork, including the importance of strong self-control. The teachers remind students to follow directions, listen to peers, take turns, exercise patience, and engage in compromise—all aspects of this critical skill.

- *Integrity:* The teachers remind the children to practice integrity by standing up for what they believe if they have strong but unpopular opinions about the playground design. This can be difficult for some 4th graders (just as some adults have difficulty speaking out about their political beliefs), so talking about integrity can become a teachable moment.

- *Embracing diversity.* As the 4th graders collect data about student preferences (using Google Forms' electronic surveys), they learn about the diversity of students' playground wants. The survey data are displayed in bar graphs so that every 4th grader can easily see students' preferences by grade. Unsurprisingly, opinions vary greatly from grade to grade. For example, although all students want a place to play basketball and kickball, the youngest students really value climbing equipment and the 8th graders want some unstructured hangout spaces. Although these differences don't surprise the adults, some students had not considered that priorities would differ according to age. Examining diversity in this very personal way sets the stage for looking at thornier diversity issues down the road. It's worth noting that racial and ethnic differences don't seem to matter much when it comes to the kinds of playground students want, suggesting a lot of commonality across categories.

- *Grit:* The nature and length of this playground design project means that students have to use grit to be successful. The project spans four months and incorporates virtually every intelligence: linguistic (reading and writing); logical-mathematical (measuring, calculating, graphing); spatial (drawing, creating three-dimensional prototypes); naturalist (considering space, weather, and climate); bodily-kinesthetic (using a variety of playground equipment and games, contemplating large and small muscles), and intrapersonal and interpersonal (planning and making presentations to peers, teachers, and outside adults). Grit comes into play when students persevere in an area that is not a strength despite frustration or failure. "The 4th graders will have to use grit to go back to the drawing board and adjust their prototypes to the wants of others," says Williams. "It will take grit to start again when a prototype needs adjustment."

This shows that the Formative Five success skills can be highlighted and taught without altering the focus of a lesson or taking significantly more time. Even if they had not been aware of the Formative Five, Williams and Roncal would have seized the creation of a playground as a rich teaching opportunity. But tomorrow's more challenging and complex world means that we need to prepare our students differently. Recognizing the importance of the Formative Five, Williams and Roncal framed their curriculum and focused their instruction to ensure that students developed the Formative Five as they learned their regular curriculum. There are times when we will explicitly teach a lesson on one of the Formative Five, but we should always look for opportunities to enhance what we are doing by designing lessons to prepare students for success in life, not just to master the task at hand.

At El Paso Leadership Academy, a charter school targeting low-income middle school students, the practice is to develop students' SEL by focusing on developing self-control, rather than simply eliciting students' adherence to rules and regulations. Founder and CEO Omar Yanar says:

Rules and regulations are only as good as the *why*. We try to avoid at all costs the authoritative stance of "this is why you must obey," but we explain how these rules benefit themselves and benefit others. This coincides with our very specific and targeted exercises to build empathy and the building of teamwork built on trust and cooperation. We focus on relationship building. When students understand how their actions can affect others, they are much more conscious of being metacognitive about their decisions. They make mistakes, but instead of outright punishment, there's a restorative practice of talking through the mistake, having students write and talk about how it affected themselves, their team, and their campus, as well as doing their best to correct the mistake, for example, an apology, fixing something broken, accepting responsibility, and explaining the situation to their parents.

Maintaining a Schoolwide Focus on SEL

Keeping SEL on the administrative agenda is essential. "I have made it a goal of mine this year for the staff to focus on students' SEL," says Mike

Flynn, principal of Timberlane Regional Middle School in Plaistow, New Hampshire. "With the help of my administrative team, each week we discuss students during our meetings. Through these discussions, we are gaining a better understanding of what is really going on in students' lives. Too often, through no fault of our own other than how we are programmed, we think students' lives outside of school are normal, when students today have more going on than ever before."

According to Flynn, strategies to support SEL often emerge from these meetings. Social-emotional learning "has been a focus through our advisory program, block scheduling, and opportunity block to building deeper and stronger relationships with our students," he says. "The relationships between students and teachers need to evolve. Students need teachers for guidance and support. More now than ever, we need to be able to show students how what we are doing in school will help them in life."

One way to address this at your next faculty meeting would be to show the three-minute video titled "The Power of Expectations" from the "How to Become Batman" episode of NPR's *Invisibilia* radio program (www.youtube.com/watch?v=hbhwlRRW_3o). The video shows that the assumptions that lab technicians had about the intelligence of the rats with which they were working had a bearing on the performance of the rats. After watching the video, have people meet in small groups to discuss how what they saw might relate to the Formative Five success skills of empathy and embracing diversity. Another strategy is to show Harvard's Implicit Association Test (IAT), taken by more than 5 million people. Everyone could bring their laptops and take the test simultaneously (if the school's Wi-Fi is strong enough); alternatively, they could take it before the session and come prepared to discuss how it felt and what they learned. Among those who have taken the test, 80 percent of people prefer younger people over older ones and 75 percent prefer white people over minorities (including 45 percent of black participants). You can find information on the test here: www.implicit.harvard.edu/implicit/demo.

In describing how she used faculty meetings, Lorinda Krey, the principal of Fairway Elementary School in Grover, Missouri, says, "every staff member was given a copy of *The Formative Five* and encouraged to read each chapter and bring it to each staff meeting. Our first year of implementation, our guidance counselor and other members of our character education committee designed and shared lesson plans. During our second year, each grade level selected its own Formative Five skill to focus on and shared the ensuing lesson with the rest of the staff."

Practices That Further Empathy Among Teachers and Students

In my *Educational Leadership* column "Building Empathy in Schools" (2018a), I offer the following steps for discussing empathy during faculty meetings:

- Begin by distinguishing between empathy and sympathy.
- Present a few controversial topics, such as Common Core standards or weekend homework assignments. Ask participants to think of three reasons someone might support or oppose each practice.
- In small groups, have participants compare their speculations with the actual reasons given by those who hold supporting or opposing views for each practice. The goal (which you'll need to state and likely restate) isn't to change minds but to offer a forum for folks to explain why they hold their beliefs—and for others to listen and learn.
- Lead the faculty in a discussion about how this activity could be done with students.

Empathy begins with understanding those who are closest to you and different from you in some way. Notes Joel Hunter, a counselor at Holland Elementary School in Springfield, Missouri: "Recently, we have been teaching the whole school to sign our Hawk PRIDE Pledge [PRIDE stands for politeness, respect, integrity, discipline, and effort] because our school houses the district's deaf students. When our music teacher does a performance, she typically incorporates either a song or a part of the song in which all of the students are signing the words."

At North Glendale Elementary School in Glendale, Missouri, SEL skills are reinforced through Unite Family Changemaker Groups, says the school's principal, Masa Massenburg-Johnson. "Every staff member is responsible for a family group comprised of students across grade levels. In this way, our very large, 600-plus student body is divided into more intimate, manageable groupings. These groups were established to ensure that all students have another adult in addition to their classroom teacher with whom they can develop a trusting relationship over the course of their time at North Glendale." The groups meet for 30 minutes each month.

Back at Fairway Elementary in Grover, Missouri, 4th grade teacher Maureen Smith developed "Got Your Backpack," a confidential weekend food program for any student in need. Students made posters, collected items, helped count and organize the items in the food pantry, and held a schoolwide assembly to promote the program. Teachers made a special effort to teach children why others need assistance by modeling empathy, wondering aloud what their circumstances could be and how they might be feeling.

Ensuring an SEL Focus in the Classroom

In visiting classes at Arundel High School in Gambrills, Maryland, I saw teachers asking the following questions:

- "What are the characteristics of good citizenship? What do good citizens do?"
- "What does it feel like not to belong? Write down three emotions you would feel."
- "Write one thing about you that gives you confidence."
- "Write something nice about the person sitting next to you."

Teaching students how to identify emotions begins with raising an awareness about emotions—what they are and how they can be identified. At Atkinson Academy in Atkinson, New Hampshire, teachers Molly

Gleason (4th grade) and Erin Lozowski (5th grade) each engage in role-plays with one student at a time while the rest of the class watches. The students' job is to discern how they think the teacher and student are feeling and explain why they believe this. Similarly, the school's counselor, Barbara Gallant, works with 2nd grade teacher Jennifer Koener and 1st grade teacher Katie Small to help students begin to infer emotions displayed by animated characters on a screen.

At Danville Elementary School in Danville, New Hampshire, librarian Beth Kisiel takes a leadership role in supporting teachers' efforts to develop empathy. She created a faculty Social, Emotional, and Academic Learning Committee (SEAL) that provides resources and activities for teachers to use with students during morning meetings and restorative circles, and holds a Literature Lunch for staff where she shares books that they could use to teach their students SEL skills.

Bart Bronk, head of University Liggett School in Grosse Pointe, Michigan, uses the play and 2016 movie adaptation of August Wilson's *Fences* to teach the school's high school students about empathy. It is difficult to like or forgive the protagonist, Troy Maxson (played by Denzel Washington in the movie). Maxson is an ex-convict who is abusive to everyone around him. Yet as the plot unfolds, Bronk notes, students begin to understand a bit why Maxson is the way that he is, perhaps showing some empathy. To complete the learning experience, moving the students through cognitive empathy, to emotional empathy, to action, Bronk has the students choose a character from the play and simulate giving the eulogy at Maxson's funeral (which is not a part of the play or movie). "These words were remarkable, but the students' reactions were sublime," notes Bronk. "As proud as I was of the students' poignant, thoughtful, and elegant efforts to celebrate Troy through the voice of another, I was even more heartened by the response of their peers in the audience. Each was captivated; some even cried. While the words being spoken belonged to members of Troy Maxson's family, the tears being shed for this tragically flawed character from Pittsburgh belonged fully, and unashamedly, to teenagers from Michigan."

"I have embedded [the Formative Five] into the culture of my classroom and my teaching," says 1st grade teacher Leslie Windler of Fairway Elementary. "I keep our five principles posted in my room and on my door, I talk about these words in my daily conversations with students, I use them as part of my classroom code of conduct, and I also embed them into daily lessons in curricular areas. I keep [the Formative Five] as a part of my daily language, so that the kids know it as more than just words."

Second grade teacher, Karen Brennan, Windler's colleague at Fairway, also emphasizes the Formative Five with her students. "I encourage grit on a daily basis rather than explicitly teach it," she says. "Any time students are challenged by their learning is the perfect time to remind them that it's not time to quit, it's time to show grit! When we're in the halls, walking by working classrooms, we also remember self-control. When someone's feelings are hurt unintentionally (or intentionally), we talk about empathy. When we're using other languages for our morning greeting and some are tempted to laugh, we revisit celebrating a diverse world. When I'm called into the hall for a moment, we remind ourselves to show integrity."

In "4 Ways to Teach Empathy in the Classroom" (2018), Roberta Brandao suggests the following four strategies for teaching empathy to students:

- Project-based learning (e.g., students work with fictional animated cartoon characters and must consider what actions would benefit them)
- Empathy maps (e.g., students place "roses" and "thorns" on a bulletin board to show the positive and negative feelings of the characters)
- Active listening (e.g., students make eye contact with the person speaking and don't interrupt)
- Reflection (e.g., students use sentence frames like "I like ____ because ____" or "I wish ____ because ____")

At Jackson Hole Middle School in Jackson Hole, Wyoming, Michelle Rooks says that she and her JHMS teammates help students develop grit by explicitly teaching mindsets. "We write essays that include defining the terms, studying statistics, and paraphrasing quotes," says Rooks. "Students weave their own anecdotes into the essays. Many of the students write about having a fixed mindset about this very writing project!" The teachers use the word *yet* to indicate that while the goal has not been reached, progress is still occurring: "We don't have a growth mindset *yet!*" Students are taught that challenges are a natural part of growth and color-code some of their assignments to indicate "I could do it myself" (green), "I'm ready to try to do it myself" (yellow), or "I need your help" (red).

At Yavneh Hebrew Academy in Los Angeles, the Formative Five success skills are taught through a mentoring system. "We have 'character mentoring' period, 20 minutes a week to focus on SEL," says headmaster Moshe Dear. "The middle school students are divided into different mentoring groups with a faculty mentor who is not their teacher. We follow the same curriculum prepared in house. Each week there is a story or scenarios followed by a series of sample discussion questions to enable the students to apply the concept. We spend six to eight weeks on a trait, before doing the next."

At Roosevelt Elementary School in Iowa City, 1st grade teacher Amy Coon, modifying the Marshmallow Test a bit, gives each student one cookie and tells students that if they wait until the end of reading, they can have another one. "I have them sit by their cookie and read a story," she says. "Then I have them complete an activity with their choice of where to work. We then discuss why or why not they waited, whether it was easy or hard to wait, and what made waiting easier." Coon has also developed rubrics for each of the Formative Five that she uses to help frame her efforts, monitor student progress, and communicate with parents.

At Grace-St. Luke's School, Williams and Roncal integrate the Formative Five into the annual 4th grade Citizenship Breakfast. Students invite an adult they consider to be a model citizen and write an essay about why they chose that person. Recently, they have begun asking students to also describe which Formative Five trait their guest best embodies.

"I propose a strategy for linking social-emotional learning to the reading curriculum already in place," writes Nancy Boyles in her *Educational Leadership* article "Learning Character from Characters" (2018, p. 71). "It involves returning to a text previously used for close reading or a book you've simply read aloud to your students. This time, ask questions related to social and emotional problem solving to begin discussions that raise students' awareness and encourage them to rethink their own responses to challenging situations."

At Danville Elementary, kids on the student council are working on being Empathy Ambassadors to other students, says Kisiel. "They will be visiting classrooms, telling students how they are ambassadors and handing out papers on which students can express ways of showing empathy." These papers are collected and then attached to an "empa-tree" on a bulletin board in the hall.

Jen Holshouser and Stephanie Bowman, teachers at St. John Lutheran School in Ellisville, Missouri, use the Formative Five to support teaching religion. They state "students examined the Formative Five principles in Bible stories and people. They noticed that the people in the Bible, especially Jesus, displayed these characteristics. Since our theme last year was to `Live like Christ,' students looked at how they could use empathy, self-control, integrity, grit, and embracing diversity in their daily lives. The students also prepared and delivered a school-wide presentation called `Holy Week and The Formative Five.' Being able to see elementary students who were acutely self-aware of their Formative Five strengths and growth areas was remarkable."

At Roosevelt Elementary, staff are encouraged to be on the lookout for student displays of the Formative Five success skills. After spotting such a display, teachers are encouraged to write the child's name and the nature of the display on a piece of paper that they then place in a jar labeled with the appropriate success skill. At weekly assemblies, the five jars are brought out and, with great fanfare, a student's name is drawn for each one. The five students come up to the stage as their names are called to receive applause and high-fives. After the drawing, the unused slips, which are color-coded by success skill, are posted to a bulletin board in the hall.

First graders in Alison Smith's class at Roosevelt learn SEL by identifying, discussing, and practicing emotions. Smith and her students engage in role-plays followed by questioning. They discuss how they know when students feel bored, angry, happy, excited, and sad. In teaching empathy, for example, a student pretends to fall, and the rest of the class is asked how they might show empathy. Or, two children participate in the role-play, one falling and the other being empathetic. "How does your classmate show empathy?" they are asked.

Third graders at Roosevelt are given a sheet of paper with various scenarios (e.g., someone dropped a lunchroom tray, someone is crying on the Buddy Bench, someone fell at recess). Children write or draw responses to explain how they knew what the person was feeling. It's important to teach students to be able to articulate what they are seeing.

One incredibly creative way to teach integrity was developed by Roosevelt Elementary teachers Jami Mundt (3rd grade), Anne Brooks (2nd grade), Hannah Owens (special education, 3–5), and Mary Biggs (5th grade). They led their students to develop "What would you do scenarios?"—situations in which students were confronted with good and bad choices (e.g., finding money on the ground, having the opportunity to look at another student's test). Students discussed the temptations and what they should do to show integrity. Teachers created a series of 30-second videos with students acting out each scenario. When the moment of decision arises, the actors turn to the camera and ask, "What would you do?" (You can see a few of the videos here: https://youtu.be/7KZmVZfzW1Q, https://youtu.be/2yFILR70kBY, https://youtu.be/T94xn48W0Is, and https://youtu.be/D1qojRlix7E.)

Producing the videos was a wonderful learning opportunity for everyone in the class, not simply those who appear on screen. In describing the creation of the scenarios for the integrity videos, for example, teacher Jami Mundt says, "There are many ways you could develop the situations with kids. I began by having a discussion with my class about moments where they felt that 'pit in your stomach' gut feeling when they were faced with a choice between right or wrong. This helps them have ownership over the videos, as well as see real-life examples of times they have experienced opportunity to show integrity."

As this chapter indicates, there is no limit to the practices that can develop SEL. From how faculty meetings are planned to the signage in the halls, from altruistic ventures to designing playgrounds or creating videos to choosing to stand in the hall to connect with as many students as possible, almost any practice can be placed within a Formative Five context to develop SEL.

The formula is simple yet powerful: I (intentionality) + T (transparency) + C (creativity) = SEL.

At Your School

- What current practices intentionally support SEL?
- How could SEL be integrated into other current practices?
- What new practices could develop SEL?

People Survey

Before reading this chapter, please take a few minutes and respond to these survey items. An explanation and scoring system appear at the end of this survey.

Please indicate your perceptions by circling SA (strongly agree), A (agree), D (disagree), or SD (strongly disagree) by each item.

1. Teacher goals should cover one school year.

    SA   A   D   SD

2. Time is routinely allocated in meetings and PD sessions for people to share a bit about themselves and what is happening in their lives.

    SA   A   D   SD

3. All faculty members are aware of the difference between honesty and integrity.

    SA   A   D   SD

4. Student efforts to help others are limited to activities done by the student body.

SA   A   D   SD

5. Student and staff discussions of politics and religion are appropriate in school.

SA   A   D   SD

6. Professional goals set by teachers and administrators are private and should only be shared with supervisors.

SA   A   D   SD

7. Staff members are encouraged to take risks and learn from their failures.

SA   A   D   SD

8. Time is spent at faculty and committee meetings to help faculty members understand, appreciate, and embrace adult diversities.

SA   A   D   SD

9. Teachers are encouraged to speak out even if they disagree with colleagues or administrators.

SA   A   D   SD

10. Teacher handbooks provide specific expectations and procedures so that teachers know how to respond in virtually every situation.

SA   A   D   SD

11. When we focus on grit, it is to help students develop it.

SA   A   D   SD

12. Learning their role is an important part of growth, so students should adhere to school rules and administrative directives without question.

SA   A   D   SD

13. During PD, we have talked about how to maintain composure while responding to an angry parent (or colleague).

SA   A   D   SD

14. Cards and celebrations to commemorate all the adults' birthdays, family additions, reconfigurations, and changes in health are routine.

SA   A   D   SD

15. Administrators are solely responsible for hiring.

SA   A   D   SD

The culture component surveys are designed to facilitate reflection and dialogue. After you have determined your score, I suggest that you answer the questions under item 1 below. Then, after two or three colleagues have also completed the survey, compare responses using the questions under item 2.

1. Does this score capture what happens in your school? Are there issues not addressed that you think are significant? Would your colleagues agree with your responses? If not, why might that be? Would your responses surprise colleagues?
2. On what items do you and your colleagues agree? When you disagree, why is that? Is there a correlation between how you see things and your position, years of experience, or another demographic factor? Were you previously aware of these different perceptions?

Scoring:

1. For items 2, 3, 5, 7, 8, 9, 13, and 14, give yourself 4 points for each SA and 3 points for each A. Then, subtract 4 points for each SD and 3 points for each D. Subtotal A= _____
2. For items 1, 4, 6, 10, 11, 12, and 15, give yourself 4 points for each SD and 3 points for each D. Subtract 4 points for each SA and 3 points for each A. Subtotal B= _____
3. Grand total (A + B) = _____

What Your Score Means:

- If your score is less than 30, your school needs to radically change how values are framed to support the people component.
- If your score is between 30–39, your school should review practices to see where improvements can be made in the people component.
- If your score is between 40–49, your school is doing a good job of supporting the people component, and you should look to see which area(s) need more attention.
- If your score is more than 50, your school is doing an excellent job of supporting the people component.

6

People

Journalist and former *60 Minutes* commentator Andy Rooney once said, "Most of us end up with no more than five or six people who remember us. Teachers have thousands of people who remember them for the rest of their lives." If we want to advance the Formative Five success skills, we must be sure that we have teachers who can effectively teach and model them. A school is only as good as the quality of its teachers, and teachers who are effective will connect with their students regardless of content or grade level.

I know this to be true personally because of my 1st grade teacher, Mrs. Helen Mayfield. First grade was many years ago, so the details are fuzzy, but I've never forgotten that she believed in me. Mrs. Mayfield didn't ignore my many foibles, but she focused on my potential and she expected me to do better. I owe much to her.

I thought it would be interesting to hear others' feelings and see if there are any commonalities. Here are some responses I received when I sent an e-mail asking people to share their recollections about a teacher who had made a significant difference in their life:

- **Masa, principal:** "One teacher who made a significant difference in my life was my 4th grade teacher Ms. Bobbie Parsons. Ms. Parsons was a powerful, brilliant, beautiful, and talented African American woman who not only empowered me to excel academically but cultivated my unique gifts and talents as well. She truly understood the importance of teaching the 'whole' child."

- **Adrianne, head of school:** "I remember my high school English teacher. She introduced me to many great authors, including Henry David Thoreau. She always called him 'Our Friend Henry David.' It was one of those quirky things that some teachers do that just endear them to you and that you remember forever. Also, when she wanted to make a point, she'd climb up on top of her desk and talk to us with her arms waving around. She was this petite woman, but when she was up on a desk, she could certainly make a point!"

- **Jane, 4th grade teacher:** "My 6th grade teacher, Mr. Reed, made a significant difference in my life. Mr. Reed was always trying new techniques with his students. His was the first class where students did not sit in neat rows. He was constantly moving us around the room and pairing us with different classmates. Mr. Reed encouraged us to read *anything*, even a comic book. He was extremely interested in each and every student. We all felt special. I try to be the teacher Mr. Reed was."

- **Joy, school leader:** "Whenever I think of why I decided to become a teacher, I think back to sitting in the room of my classics teacher, Dr. Greg Knittel, or 'Doc' as we called him. He was, in my 10th grader eyes, erudite beyond measure. I looked up to him, however, not only because he was brilliant but also—and more so—because of the kind of man he was. He was funny, he was authentic, and he clearly cared about what kind of people we were becoming as much as about our knowledge of Latin and Greek declensions. He inspired me to become a teacher because I wanted to be like him, to have significance in the lives of others, as he'd had in mine. Quite literally, he changed my life."

- **Vivian, a former teacher and current writer:** "I don't remember the grade, but Miss Bremmer asked me why I had chosen a particular word in a story I was writing. I told her I hadn't used the word I wanted to use because I didn't know how to spell it. That day, when the other students were at recess, my teacher taught me how to look up a word in the dictionary, even if I wasn't sure about how to spell it."

Amazing teachers like the ones mentioned above can serve as the basis for a powerful professional development activity. Once just prior to the start of the school year, I asked teachers to think back to a few teachers who have had a powerful influence on their lives and to write two or three adjectives that describe them. Teachers then gathered in small groups and shared the characteristics. Regardless of the grade or subject taught, the teachers that faculty selected are those who knew them, who held high expectations for them, and who encouraged and prodded them. After this sharing, I asked the teachers to take a few minutes and think of what they can do with their students so that they might be named in this sort of exercise 20 or 30 years hence. "What are you already doing that you need to continue?" I asked. "What can you begin? What can you discard because it keeps you from being this kind of teacher?"

In "How Kids Learn Resilience," Paul Tough notes that if we want students to succeed, particularly those who come from challenging home environments, we must convey the following message: "You're safe; life is going to be fine. Let down your guard; the people around you will protect you and provide for you. Be curious about the world; it's full of fascinating surprises" (2016). Not surprisingly, these same messages produce an effective adult team. In "What Google Learned from Its Quest to Build the Perfect Team," Charles Duhigg (2016) notes that "Google's data indicated that psychological safety, more than anything else, was critical to making a team work."

The Importance of Trust

Teaching SEL skills requires a culture of trust, both within classrooms and throughout the school. Because there is no scope-and-sequence script for teaching the Formative Five, educators must work and learn alongside others who are confronting the same issues; trust is necessary in this context for educators to take risks and tread into uncomfortable waters as they develop their SEL skills.

Students are good observers, and they see whether we practice what we preach. A teacher's marvelous lesson on empathy can be totally negated by a single thoughtless comment. According to Berman, Chaffee, and Sarmiento (2018), "Students learn by what they hear and observe as adults relate to students and other adults. They notice whether adults' actions are congruent with their words and whether adults demonstrate the same social and emotional competencies they expect of students" (p. 9).

A schoolwide pursuit of the Formative Five creates synergy. To this end, we should consider how the Formative Five can be reflected in three discrete areas: hiring, collegiality, and professional development (PD).

Hiring

Administrators want to hire teachers who both possess and are comfortable teaching each of the Formative Five success skills, although empathy and embracing diversity move to the front of the line when considering candidates. Schools and districts can structure the hiring process to create opportunities for learning about these qualities.

Most important, a team should be involved in hiring. Administrators should have the final decision because they are ultimately responsible for what happens in the school, but teacher involvement and engagement throughout the hiring process is essential. When people who occupy different hierarchical positions sit around the table, roles and processes must be clearly explained to avoid confusion. My preference is to convene an interviewing team of two or three others with whom the new hire would be working most closely. I'd say to them, "Together, we will decide who's the best fit. I can veto your choice, but I will not hire someone unless we are all enthusiastic about the decision." Then, I would ask the team what sort of qualities we're seeking. Beyond hiring a good teacher, what specific talents, interests, or experiences do we want?

We need to recognize that our natural tendency is to hire people who look like us and have the same kinds of experiences we do. Articulating that bias early in the hiring process and asking people to be self-aware and guard against this tendency is helpful. Having a range of backgrounds and experiences on the interviewing team is important.

In determining the perceptiveness and empathy of candidates, principal Brett Abbotts of Roosevelt Elementary School in Council Bluffs, Iowa, begins with the following question: "When completing your research of our district and school, what are some things that you noticed?" During the interview, candidates are asked to respond to the following sentence stems:

- "When a student in my class struggles with integrity, I will _____."
- "In my classroom, I will model empathy by _____."
- "Students display self-control by _____."

"All teachers hired at Roosevelt receive a copy of *The Formative Five*," says Abbotts. "They complete a six-week book study with me and my school counselor where we emphasize the success skills and how they are directly applicable in the classroom."

Hiring with Embracing Diversity in Mind

All new hires should embrace diversity regardless of a school's demographics, mission, or location. A school may seem homogenous because everyone looks similar, but many aspects of diversity are not determined visually. As with scratching a palimpsest, one only need look beneath the surface and a diversity of diversities—religion, socio-economic status, race, political persuasion, sexual orientation—will appear. In perusing candidates' resumes and cover letters, look for experiences that suggest an embracing of diversity. Has the candidate been involved in an organization that advocates for disenfranchised groups? Does the candidate routinely venture out of his or her zip code? During the interview, explicitly ask candidates how they would respond to diversity-related hypothetical scenarios (e.g., "A student complains that a peer has called her a racial pejorative. What do you do?" "A student asks why Confederate monuments are being removed. How do you respond?" "What would you do if a new student visibly looked different —skin color, clothing—than the rest of the class?"). Extra credit goes to candidates whose answers include soliciting colleagues' thoughts.

"We want all students to bring their identity with them to Burroughs," says Andy Abbott, head of school at John Burroughs School in St. Louis, Missouri. "Leave no part of yourself at the door." Asking both teacher and administrative candidates what this might mean and how they would respond in their role at the school could be a good way to elicit their understanding and perceptions of diversity.

Hiring with Empathy in Mind

Ask candidates to reflect on a student with whom they worked who was struggling, and then ask what they did to help that student. Cognitive and emotional empathy are important—we want teachers to understand how others are feeling and to feel along with them—but they are not enough. We want teachers whose actionable empathy will cause them to take action in support of students. Listening to candidates as they share their feelings and perspectives should be a part of any strategy.

It's also a good idea to ask potential new staff how they would react to real-life situations in which people are in conflict (e.g., a parent

who is unhappy about a teacher comes to school to demand an imme-
diate conference, or an altercation occurs on the playground). Listening
will be part of any empathic response. Candidates with strong empathy will automatically include what people were seeing and how they
were feeling in their answer. Paul M. Fanuele, the executive principal of
Arlington High School in Lagrangeville, New York, says candidates at his
school must teach a demonstration lesson before being hired: "During
the lesson we look for relationship building and connection with our
students. One simple way to observe this is if the candidate uses student
names during the lesson."

Asking "What's the difference between sympathy and empathy?"
and "How would you teach your students empathy?" will yield insights
into the candidate's experiences and attitudes. Although these questions
are relevant for any candidate, they may have even more significance
when asked of a subject-matter specialist who has deep expertise in a
curriculum area. Regardless of what content or skill is taught, a goal
should be to help students become aware of and understand others'
perceptions.

Hiring with Integrity in Mind

Ask candidates to share an example of a time when they took a
position that ran counter to the peer group or authority. Once they have
shared an example, ask them how others reacted. A question like "Is
there ever a time when dishonesty is appropriate?" will provide valuable
insight into a candidate's experiences and philosophy around honesty
and integrity. If a candidate quickly responds no, you may wish to push
further: "What about someone who has a certain prognosis of death. Is
it acceptable to give that person false hope?" (There are many possible
answers; the goal is simply to elicit thinking and values.)

Another strategy is to ask candidates to name three historical figures they admire and explain why. You are looking to see if someone
is identified due to integrity—speaking out even when it's at a personal cost. A follow-up question might be, "How would you teach your

students integrity?" Candidates should understand that students who demonstrate integrity may not always conform to class expectations or teacher's rules.

Hiring with Self-Control in Mind

Discuss the Marshmallow Test (see p. 33) with candidates. Ask if they would have had the self-control to resist eating the marshmallow at age 4. Then, more generally, ask how the candidate learned self-control. It is also wise to probe what candidates think the relationship is between classroom rules and self-control, particularly to see if they differentiate between external and internal controls and compliance versus personal responsibility. Questions such as "How can faculty members model self-control for students?", "What are the marshmallows in our adult lives?", and "What's the relationship between self-control developed from incentives versus self-control stemming from punishments?" will further uncover a candidate's educational biases.

Hiring with Grit in Mind

Encourage candidates to share when they learned grit, a time when they used it, and the techniques they employed. Have they ever intentionally shared their grit experiences with students? Ask, "Why do some educators think it's unfair to view grit as a positive factor?" Whether or not they agree, they need to understand that some people feel that focusing on grit discounts a student's personal or environmental challenges. Have them explain how the practices they use to develop grit in students might differ for kids who are used to succeeding versus those for whom frustration is the norm. Be sure to also ask if students' effort, trajectory, or grit should be factors in their grades.

The Importance of Collegiality

Significant problems in a school are best addressed by teams that use SEL skills to work well together and capitalize on one another's strengths and perspectives. In his *Forbes* article "What Great Problem Solvers Do Differently," Joseph Folkman notes the importance of having excellent interpersonal skills. "Great solutions come from integrating your ideas with those of others to find a better solution," he writes. "Excellent problem solvers build networks and know how to collaborate with other people and teams. They are skilled in bringing people together and sharing knowledge and information. A key skill for great problem solvers is that they are trusted by others" (2018).

Charles Duhigg (2016) writes: "To prepare students for that complex world, business schools around the country have revised their curriculums to emphasize team-focused learning" and "In the best teams, members listen to one another and show sensitivity to feelings and needs." "Good leaders try to use questions more than statements," writes Adam Bryant (2017) in *The New York Times* "so that their employees take ownership of their roles rather than simply take orders from the CEO."

The need for a personal connection is true in athletics, too. St. Louis Baseball Cardinals' manager Mike Schildt stated that his goal is "continual collaboration," and spent the off-season meeting with team members and front office staff. During his first season as manager, he began "Ball Talk," optional daily meetings in which players could come to discuss strategy and talk about the previous game. This tapped into the players need to learn and connect with others. "Eventually, the meetings were packed with players, brimming with discussion," he said (Goold, 2019, p. B4).

I have visited enough schools to recognize that every single one is unique. Ages and demographics of students and staff vary from school to school, as does allocation and use of resources. What all high-quality schools have in common, however, is a collegial faculty of teachers and administrators who learn together and view one another as resources. Collegiality puts relationships and synergy at the heart of a school. In his book *Improving Schools from Within*, Roland Barth (1990) sets forth the following four core components of collegiality:

- Teachers discussing students
- Teachers developing curriculum together
- Teachers teaching one another
- Teachers observing one another

To these, I add a fifth: Teachers and administrators learning together. In implementing the Formative Five, I recommend the creation of one or more faculty committees to help ensure that collegiality contributes to and benefits the school—perhaps a separate committee for each of the success skills, or maybe a committee focused on monitoring and sharing student progress.

Here are some examples of how Barth's components of collegiality can be used within a SEL and Formative Five context.

Teachers Discussing Students

Students' behaviors can change depending on their surroundings, so there is much to be gained from discussions among staff who see kids in different contexts (e.g., specialty teachers, aides, security officers, bus drivers, lunch supervisors). These discussions will reinforce everyone's awareness of the Formative Five.

Discussing students invariably includes what students understand and how we know that. Consequently, the question of assessment—of what and how we should measure student success—is one all SEL educators must address. "Data doesn't have to reduce our students to a number, but the way we treat our students can," writes Christine Torres (2019). "What if we designed assessments that didn't just test students on a standards-based concept or the right answer, but also showed their abilities and understandings of their communities and cultures?" (p. 2). Think of the benefits that would stem from discussing student progress in the Formative Five.

Teachers Developing Curriculum Together

Faculty teams and committees should meet to evaluate and create curriculum that addresses each of the Formative Five. There are quite a few organizations that produce SEL curriculum, and some are quite good, such as the Collaborative for Academic, Social, and Emotional Learning (CASEL), but there is merit in teachers at a school collaborating and constructing their own materials, which yields a strong sense of ownership. "Developing curriculum" need not mean producing scope-and-sequence charts or binders filled with information; sometimes it means engaging in conversations that result in strategies. For example, let's say teachers are frustrated that their students don't show more integrity in difficult situations with their peers. In developing strategies to address this, share the following quotes at a faculty meeting and have people meet in small groups to discuss the implications (Killinger, 2010):

- "Integrity obliges us to become personally involved in actively doing something to right a wrong" (p. 14).
- "In today's world, personal and professional integrity are being put to the test. Two factors of particular concern are *a move away from relationships*, leading to alienation and impersonal detachment, and the *seduction of greed*, which is not only fed by stress-related economic and psychological insecurities but by a heightened preoccupation with security itself" (p. x).
- "Recognizing the *importance of relationship*" is the key to strengthen values that support integrity (p. xii).

Teachers Teaching One Another

As virtually every educator remembers from student teaching, the best way to learn something is to teach it, so teaching the Formative

Five skills to colleagues is quite valuable. Because I believe that faculty committees are the engines for growth, there were always three or more committees meeting at my school, mostly in the afternoon but occasionally in the morning. These committees learned about and developed strategies to address multiple intelligences, racial issues, parent communication, curriculum continuity, and student assessment. Most of these groups are chaired by teachers who would periodically share their committees' progress at faculty meetings.

Teachers Observing One Another

In my experience, this is the most difficult principle of collegiality to bring to life because it runs counter to educational norms. I suggest teachers work in groups of three, with two teachers observing a third teacher, and rotating so that everyone sees and is seen. The three teachers meet after each observation to share their insights and questions. Each meeting begins with the teacher who was being observed sharing reflections on the lesson—what worked and what could be improved upon. The task of the two observing teachers is to offer praise and questions in a 2:1 ratio (that is, two commendations for every question asked). This formula may feel artificial, but it forces everyone to focus on the positive and not take good teaching for granted.

Atul Gawande (2011), a surgeon and author, proposes that everyone would benefit from having a coach. "The concept of a coach is slippery," he writes. "Coaches are not teachers, but they teach. They're not your boss—in professional tennis, golf, and skating, the athlete hires and fires the coach—but they can be bossy. They don't even have to be good at the sport. Mainly, they observe, they judge, and they guide."

Gawande (2011) references data on teacher coaches that are quite powerful:

California researchers in the early nineteen-eighties conducted a five-year study of teacher-skill development in eighty schools and noticed something interesting. Workshops led teachers to use new skills in the classroom only ten per cent of the time. Even when a practice session with demon-strations and personal feedback was added, fewer than twenty per cent made the change. But when coaching was introduced—when a colleague watched them try the new skills in their own classroom and provided sug-gestions—adoption rates passed ninety per cent.

Teachers and Administrators Learning Together

Teachers and administrators must take equal responsibility for implementing the Formative Five; this isn't something that can be dele-gated or assigned. Principals need to leave their comfort zones and share what is easy and difficult for them. In collegial faculty and committee meetings, teams of administrators and teachers can discuss such central questions as "How best can we implement the Formative Five?" "What traditions can we create that will reinforce the five skills?" "How can the halls and walls support the Formative Five and how should student progress be recorded and shared?" "How can we support teachers who are trying new strategies and leaving their comfort zones?"

Using Book Groups to Facilitate Collegiality

Every school should have at least one faculty book group. Meeting on a regular basis to discuss a book, a chapter from a book, or an article —perhaps article group sounds less daunting?—is a great way to gain new insights while connecting with and learning from colleagues.

Fanuele of Arlington High School in New York shares that groups at his school have read the following books over the past few years: *Mind-set* (Dweck, 2007), *Drive* (Pink, 2009), *The Other Wes Moore* (Moore, 2011), *Habitudes* (Elmore, 2011), and *Learning to Choose, Choosing to Learn* (Anderson, 2016). At New City School, we have read such books as *Frames of Mind* (Gardner, 1983), *I Know Why the Caged Bird Sings* (Angelou, 1969), *Quiet* (Cain, 2012), *Warriors Don't Cry* (Beals, 1994), *Emotional Intelligence* (Goleman, 1995), and *The No. 1 Ladies' Detec-tive Agency* (Smith, 2002). At Littlestown High School in Pennsylvania, faculty read *Leading the New Literacies* (Jacobs, 2014) in preparation for their move to 1:1 devices. "While all staff read the book, they did not read it all at the same time," says Lori Stollar, director of curriculum and technology. "The reading was phased in with groups of teachers as each cohort prepared to shift their teaching practice to leverage technology for learning, coinciding with the rollout of devices." Tricia Diebold of Special School District in St. Louis reports that faculty there are about to read *Dare to Lead* (Brown, 2018) and recently read *Witnessing Whiteness* (Tochluk, 2010). In Karaj, Iran, headmaster Bahram Ghaseminejad of the Kourosh Elementary School adds TED Talks and movies to the mix: Faculty at the school have watched Ken Robinson's TED Talks and speeches by Carol Dweck, Angela Duckworth, and Daniel Pink as well as the movies *Life Is Beautiful* and *Dead Poets Society.* He also uses music and music videos with his faculty to encourage reflection and dialogue such as Pink Floyd's "Another Brick in the Wall" (part two) where they say, "We don't need no education," and John Lennon's "Imagine," which speaks to diversity, care, and peace. Think of the enthusiasm and creativity that could be generated if students were asked to identify music or music videos which esteemed empathy, self-control, integrity, embracing diversity, or grit.

These group discussions won't always be easy; in fact, they shouldn't be. If we are to capitalize on others' experiences and ideas, there will invariably be times when we are moved out of our comfort zones. Just as we don't grow as much from our successes as from our failures, we don't learn when everyone agrees with us. Daniel Coyle (2018) refers to this phenomenon when he writes that cooperation "does not simply descend out of the blue. It is a group muscle that is built according to a specific pattern of repeated interaction, and that pattern is always the same: a circle of people engaged in the risky, occasionally painful, ultimately rewarding process of being vulnerable together" (p. 113). Over time, we will develop trust and an appreciation for these differences, and the result will be growth, which ultimately benefits our students and ourselves.

Professional Development

We need to remember that adults and children learn in similar ways; whether the learner is 8, 28, 48, or older, attention spans and creature comforts must be taken into consideration. Learning should be active, breaks should be provided, and snacks (both healthy and not-so) should be available. Educators already have too much on their plates and not enough time to get everything done, so leaders must begin by motivating and establishing that learning to teach SEL is an important priority.

But beyond its value, we must ensure that our PD offerings are engaging to staff. No one wants to hear edicts or to be read information, even if it is important. Asking these questions will elicit rich dialogues among faculty members:

- "Why is SEL important?"
- "What are we currently doing for SEL?"
- "What worries you about implementing SEL?"
- "How can we develop students' SEL?"

Educators should be able to plan collaboratively and create strategies that work in their communities and schools. To facilitate faculty receptivity, consider canceling a faculty meeting and giving staff an alternate assignment—taking the hour to have a conversation about SEL with someone they don't know well in the building, for example. Or ask everyone to leave the building and talk to someone who is not part of the school community. Place these assignments in the context of empathy and listening and make sure staff spend the subsequent meeting sharing what they learned and what surprised them.

Professional development focused on SEL is different from that which addresses academics because we, the adults, need to develop our SEL skills, too. Teachers and administrators need the expectation and opportunity that they will participate in the same kinds of activities as will the students. School leaders—regardless of their titles—can facilitate this by stepping forward and visibly participating.

Here are some relatively nonthreatening ways to begin to engage faculty members in developing their Formative Five success skills, each of which could constitute the focus of a faculty meeting or PD session:

- Discuss the *Atlantic* article "Why Rich Kids Are So Good at the Marshmallow Test" (Calarco, 2018; available here: https://www.theatlantic.com/family/archive/2018/06/marshmallow-test/561779/).

- Discuss the book *Material World: A Global Family Portrait* (1995) by Peter Menzel and Charles Mann. What varieties of living conditions might you see in your community and how can your school reflect them?

- Watch Brené Brown's 2010 TED Talk on vulnerability (available here: https://www.ted.com/talks/brene_brown_on_vulnerability?language=en). How is vulnerability important in our lives, particularly as we pursue the Formative Five?

- Watch Philip Zimbardo's 2008 TED Talk on "the psychology of evil" (available here: https://www.ted.com/talks/philip_zimbardo_on_the_psychology_of_evil/transcript?language=en). What surprised you about the TED Talk? Are there any takeaways you can apply to your school?

- Facilitate a discussion on how integrity is or is not manifested in everyday life. Read books such as *The Perilous Adventures of the Cowboy King: A Novel of Teddy Roosevelt and His Times* by Jerome Charyn (2019), *Sing, Unburied, Sing* by Jesmyn Ward (2017), or *The Soul of America* by Jon Meacham (2018). Longer but quite powerful books could include *These Truths: A History of the United States* (2018) by Jill Lepore, *Frederick Douglass: Prophet of Freedom* (2018) by David Blight, or *All the King's Men* (1946) by Robert Penn Warren.

- Watch the animated video *The Atlantic Slave Trade in Two Minutes* (2015) by Andrew Kahn and Jamelle Bouie (available here: www.slate.com/articles/life/the_history_of_american_slavery/2015/06/animated_interactive_of_the_history_of_the_atlantic_slave_trade.html), which shows the route of 20,528 ships carrying slaves to the New World from 1545 through 1860.

What surprised you? Why did it take so long for the vestiges of slavery to disappear?

- Read and discuss the 2018 *New York Times* article "New Year's Day Is Also Emancipation Day" by Jesse L. Jackson Sr. (available here: https://www.nytimes.com/2018/12/30/opinion/new -years-day-emancipation-proclamation.html). Do you like this idea? Why is it so little known?

- Ask all staff to set a goal of venturing out of their comfort zones over the next week. At the next meeting, have everyone write about their experience, including whether they were successful, on a 3 x 5 card *without sharing it with anyone.* Allow a few minutes for folks to meet in small groups and share whether this was difficult and what strategies they used. (Sharing what they did remains optional.)

- Read and discuss the 2018 *Washington Post* column "For College Admissions, Let's Value Grit Over GPA" by Mitch Daniels (available here: https://www.washingtonpost.com/opinions/ for-college-admissions-lets-value-grit-over-gpas/2018/11/28/ 8aa1c9c4-ed09-11e8-8679-934a2b33be52_story.html?utm_ term=.2064eb7a5a43). Do you agree with the article? Will technological advances affect the article's conclusions?

- Discuss the 2016 *Cleveland Plain Dealer* article "'Diversity Is Being Invited to the Party; Inclusion Is Being Asked to Dance,' Verna Myers Tells Cleveland Bar" by Janet H. Cho (available here: https://articles.cleveland.com/business/index.ssf/2016/05/ diversity_is_being_invited_to.amp). What does this mean? Can you give examples in your community for which this is a good metaphor?

It's important that teachers and administrators feel valued. It's too easy to take this for granted, especially with long-standing and high-flying employees. Creating a narrative that celebrates employees results in positive feelings (and likely greater productivity). Early in my time at New City, we were experiencing too much teacher turnover. We increased salaries, and we also established a tradition of awarding Griffin Pins to all employees at their five-year anniversaries. This took place at the annual school picnic, in front of hundreds of cheering students, parents, and colleagues. Prior to the picnic, I solicited positive comments about each recipient from peers and read them aloud as the pins were given. Even on a hot June afternoon, many staff members blushed when they heard the kind things that their colleagues said about them. People are what determines the quality of our schools and the experiences of our students.

At Your School

- In what ways is SEL a factor in hiring?
- How is SEL part of PD?
- How are adults developing their SEL?

Narrative Survey

Before reading this chapter, please take a few minutes and respond to these survey items. An explanation and scoring system appear at the end of this survey.

Please indicate your perceptions by circling SA (strongly agree), A (agree), D (disagree), or SD (strongly disagree) by each item.

1. A school's narrative is stories and oral recounting.

    SA   A   D   SD

2. The best story is a brief story.

    SA   A   D   SD

3. An administrator or teacher can create a tradition.

    SA   A   D   SD

4. Staff members, interests, and their achievements are publicly visible in the school's hall or common areas.

    SA   A   D   SD

5. Faculty meetings should be held on an as-needed basis when important information needs to be shared.

    SA   A   D   SD

6. Our school's values are affirmed at student assemblies.

    SA   A   D   SD

7. Each year our new staff T-shirt delivers a powerful message.

    SA   A   D   SD

8. Everyone works hard so it's not fair to cite someone's extra effort at a faculty meeting.

    SA   A   D   SD

9. Administrators should craft the messages in our narrative.

    SA   A   D   SD

10. A school's mission and its principles are cited at every parent event.

    SA   A   D   SD

11. We give as much energy planning the end of meetings as we do the beginning.

    SA   A   D   SD

12. We cannot control the community narrative about our school, so we should not spend much energy trying to do so.

    SA   A   D   SD

13. Teachers sharing strategies with one another is not appropriate for faculty meetings.

    SA   A   D   SD

14. Which adults talk with which other adults is part of a school's narrative.

SA   A   D   SD

15. Explaining the history and traditions of our school is part of every new employee's orientation.

SA   A   D   SD

The culture component surveys are designed to facilitate reflection and dialogue. After you have determined your score, I suggest that you answer the questions under item 1 below. Then, after two or three colleagues have also completed the survey, compare responses using the questions under item 2.

1. Does this score capture what happens in your school? Are there issues not addressed that you think are significant? Would your colleagues agree with your responses? If not, why might that be? Would your responses surprise colleagues?
2. On what items do you and your colleagues agree? When you disagree, why is that? Is there a correlation between how you see things and your position, years of experience, or another demographic factor? Were you previously aware of these different perceptions?

Scoring:

1. For items 3, 4, 6, 7, 10, 11, and 15, give yourself 4 points for each SA and 3 points for each A. Subtract 4 points for each SD and 3 points for each D. Subtotal A= _____
2. For items 1, 2, 5, 8, 9, 12, 13, and 14, give yourself 4 points for each SD and 3 points for each D. Subtract 4 points for each SA and 3 points for each A. Subtotal B= _____
3. Grand total (A + B) = _____

What Your Score Means:

- If your score is less than 30, your school needs to radically change how values are framed to support the narrative component.
- If your score is between 30–39, your school should review practices to see where improvements can be made in the narrative component.
- If your score is between 40–49, your school is doing a good job of supporting the narrative component, and you should look to see which area(s) need more attention.
- If your score is more than 50, your school is doing an excellent job of supporting the narrative component.

7

Narrative

What's unique about your school's culture? Why should people choose to work at or send their children to your school? Do you focus on history or the future? Our thoughts are inevitably framed by the narrative surrounding your school. A lot of that cultural narrative is intentional, created by committees, PR firms, and graphic designers; some of it, however, may be both unintentional and corrosive, the result of a thousand paper-cut conversations. Regardless of the position they hold, strong leaders recognize the power of narrative and work to fashion it by consciously creating traditions and habits that foster the culture they value.

In an interview in *Strategy + Business*, Howard Gardner points out how stories can bring people together or push them apart. He says, "I make a big distinction, though, between inclusionary and exclusionary stories. And this is an interesting notion from the point of view of business. Inclusionary stories try to incorporate more and more people; exclusionary ones pit people against one another" (Kurtzman, 1999). How this can occur in schools is captured by Tamera Musiowsky-Borneman when she notes in an e-mail how language can intentionally be used to exemplify a community's values:

Administrators can share personal stories in conversations or at assemblies that bring forth a time in which it was necessary to be especially open-minded or empathetic toward a student or staff member. These stories can then be showcased in words or photos on hall display boards as an ongoing exhibition in which members of the school community are reminded of the common language that supports a positive culture. In addition to this, staff members can use language of support with each other and ask thought-provoking questioning techniques with their students.

Narrative takes us beyond the here and now and helps us envision history, rationale, intention, and possibility. Culture is framed and illuminated by the traditions and rituals that comprise narrative and create the organization's story. From the dunking booth at the school picnic in which the principal routinely plummets into the water and arises to students' cheers, to everyone getting an ice cream treat on the last day of school, to beginning faculty meetings by noting birthdays, and to opening assemblies with the school song, traditions form the narrative that is culture.

Far more than we might think, we observe and record (even if we are not aware of doing so) and are programmed to pick up on these kinds of traditions and narratives to define our group or organization and our membership. Writing in *She Has Her Mother's Laugh*, Carl Zimmer describes a test that his daughter took to determine how well young children could solve problems compared to chimpanzees. Zimmer notes, "We are well adapted for inheriting culture. We pass genes down through generations, but we also pass down recipes, songs, knowledge, and rituals" (2018, p. 447). The results of his daughter's test indicated the power of culture: Young children over-imitate, copying needless steps they have observed, whereas chimpanzees ignore superfluous steps.

What we wear to school can be part of the narrative. On the day that I visited Arundel High in Gambrills, Maryland, many staff members were wearing black shirts with a big kelly-green letter *A* on the front for *Arundel*. The back of the shirt had *ALL IN* written in huge uppercase letters. This, says principal Gina Davenport, is "to remind everyone that at Arundel we put all our resources in the pot because each student is a winning hand." When I visited at Fairway Elementary in Grover, Missouri, several staff members were wearing white Fairway Eagles T-shirts with the Formative Five success skills listed inside a red heart on the chest. At New City School, we had the tradition of ending every August professional development session by giving each staff member a New City T-shirt reflecting the theme for the year: "Got Grit!" "A Multiple Intelligences School" "Where Kids Come First!" and "Good Failures" were some examples. Staff members wearing shirts with a message make a strong narrative.

Narrative traditions can be seen in everything from the acronyms and idiosyncratic aphorisms we use (I used to like saying "At New City School, flexibility is our *F*-word") to routines during standardized testing week, to why, when, and how students' caregivers are summoned to a meeting. Often an organization's narrative and culture seem conterminous. Herb Kelleher gained fame by leading Southwest, a small, local airline, to become a national carrier, and doing it in a way that was fun and respectful. In the 2019 *Forbes* article "20 Reasons Why Herb Kelleher Was One of the Most Beloved Leaders of Our Time," Ken and Jackie Freiberg analyze Kelleher's speeches, annual reports, and conversations and note: "You will find that he constantly showered the people of Southwest with gratitude because that's the way he felt. He treated them with dignity and respect. He empathized with their failures and grief. He celebrated their victories. And, he showed them how much he admired them, valued them and loved them as people, not just workers." "It is a culture that recognizes the value of the individual," says Kelleher himself, "which encourages an entrepreneurial spirit, which helps people to find the career that makes them happy, and which encourages people to have fun at work. These are the very reasons for our success."

Of all the aspects of culture, narrative may be the most elusive—and the most powerful. It is elusive because much, perhaps all, of it is shared informally, passed along while standing in line or chatting at the coffee maker, or exists only in vibrant memories. Sometimes, of course, narrative is part of a presentation or mantra. Occasionally it can be part of a story, almost a myth, about leaders or employees who are admired (or eschewed). Regardless, what the narrative does is frame expectations and influence behaviors. As John Coleman (2013) says,

> Any organization has a unique history—a unique story. And the ability to unearth that history and craft it into a narrative is a core element of culture creation. The elements of that narrative can be formal—like Coca-Cola, which dedicated an enormous resource to celebrating its heritage and even has a World of Coke museum in Atlanta—or informal, like those stories about how Steve Jobs' early fascination with calligraphy shaped the aesthetically oriented culture at Apple.

Traditions are an important part of culture. Consider, for example, Jobs's routine during presentations before hundreds of media and employees of saying, "Oh yeah, there's one more thing" before unveiling some stunning technological feature. Everyone knew to wait with anticipation for that one more thing. This part of Jobs's narrative told everyone that at Apple, innovation is the norm. It was a statement about the culture at Apple, and Jobs was telling employees that they were special because they worked there (Isaacson, 2012).

The need to organize reality into an image that can be shared is so strong that it can transcend a lack of paper. In *Frederick Douglass: Prophet of Freedom*, David Blight states, "Slaves on plantations could not own much of anything—land, tools, the clothes on their bodies, even their own children or their sense of the future. But they could at times and under certain circumstances own the sounds and rhythms, the melodies and the lyrics, in the air as the great slave-driven machine of the Wye plantation refueled for the next month's production" (2018, p. 32).

Sometimes words provide images that make concepts easier to understand and remember. This is evident in the advice that pediatrician Alison Nash offers to new parents. "As a way to encourage language development," she says, she tells them that they are the "tour guides of their child's life . . . use as many words as you can as you go about daily activities, give your child many experiences as you can. . . . the more they hear and see, the more they will say and do."

Individual words and phrases can be very powerful. For example, in "Spreading Social-Emotional Learning Across All Schools," Evie Blad writes: "Rather than introducing a new program that teachers [at Tacoma, Washington, schools] would see as just another mandate, the initiative started with administrators, who spent a whole year 'braiding' duplicative school programs together, eliminating ones that weren't necessary, and establishing a common vision" (2018, p. 8). The word *braiding* creates a positive image that may help ameliorate educators' concerns. At Sandown Elementary in New Hampshire, faculty often repeat the phrase "Learning is a form of diversity." Juxtaposing learning and diversity reminds educators that children learn differently because of who they are, not due to what they have decided. At Edgefield Primary School in Singapore, principal Michel Saw says that staff begin every meeting by sharing thanks and appreciation for the good things that colleagues have done. They practice GST, he says: "To Greet everyone cheerfully with a Smile and to say Thank you."

Narrative includes who hangs out together and who talks to whom. It's important for teachers and especially administrators to understand that everyone is watching where they stand and with whom they chat; everything they do sets a precedent. When I was a principal, every school day at dismissal time, I made it a point to stand outside the building, step out of my comfort zone, and initiate conversations with parents and other caregivers with whom I may not otherwise have the opportunity to engage.

The power of narrative can also be seen in the actions we choose *not* to take. Many of us know that George Washington voluntarily stepped down after two terms, creating a norm that lasted 150 years. But just as significant is the precedent he set by what he did *not* do. In *These Truths: A History of the United States*, Jill Lepore (2018) describes Washington's first inauguration as president in 1789: "Nearly everything Washington did set a precedent. What would have happened if he had decided, before taking that oath of office, to emancipate his slaves?" Sadly, he did not—Washington owned 123 slaves when he died in 1799. The narrative that would have been created by him releasing his slaves would have rippled far, far beyond the freedom given to those individuals, perhaps even saving the country from Civil War.

Implementing Ideas and Strategies Related to Narrative

Jennifer Roberts, principal of Essex Elementary School in Essex, Massachusetts, uses music at the start of schoolwide meetings to support a consistent narrative. "We hold schoolwide meetings six or seven times per year where a grade level focuses on one of our core values and models it in some way," she says. "We include music performed by students and fun activities to support the values."

Thor Kvande, head of Grace-St. Luke's School in Memphis, Tennessee, uses success skills to help shape his school's narrative. "I introduce the Formative Five to our candidates as our character education program and part of what differentiates us from other schools," he says. "I emphasize that we focus on the whole child, and that means we spend time thinking about not only the academics, but the social-emotional aspect of development . . . this is a big part of why our kids are known far and wide as 'good kids.'"

Somewhat similarly, at every parent meeting that I held at New City School, I always began by noting our school's principles: academics, ambience, and diversity. In my initial years at the school, we even put the three principles on our stationery and featured it in signage in the halls. Later, after working with a marketing committee, we changed our terms and I began meetings by routinely referring to "our pillars: academics, the personal intelligences, diversity beyond the numbers, and joyful learning." Those principles became part of our narrative because I made a point of saying them over and over.

Recently I was part of a search committee that interviewed three candidates who had applied to be a principal, and we were all struck by how one of them referred to his present school's students as "scholars."

He routinely used that term: "After lunch," he'd say, "our scholars are free to go outside or study," or "Teachers meet weekly to talk about their scholars," or "Scholars' parents know that I'm available to meet whenever they want to talk." This was a powerful part of his narrative, reminding listeners at every turn that he had high academic expectations for students. Simply hearing him use the word *scholar* so much influenced how we viewed him.

Narrative can capture a school's history in order to frame the future. "We are a relatively young school, so we spend a lot of time sharing the founding story of the school," says Bill Hudson of Mounds Park Academy in St. Paul, Minnesota. "We are lucky enough to have several founding teachers still on staff who are willing to tell the story. It is a part of our new employee orientation, new board member orientation, and new parent orientation. We also tell it once a year to students when we celebrate the school's founding (the day the articles of incorporation were signed) with a pancake breakfast served by the board and administration."

At New City School, we used to periodically feature photos of each of our staff members (not just teachers) on the bulletin board in the front hall, near the school's main entrance. When we implemented the multiple intelligences in the school, we asked staff members to identify their strongest intelligences and posted them alongside their pictures; other times we had them list their hobbies or their favorite foods. Some schools feature a different teacher in each family newsletter. The buzz that actions like this create becomes a powerful piece of the school community narrative.

Staff and Faculty Meetings

What we call something can create a narrative identity that changes perceptions and behavior. "We got rid of the term 'staff meeting' and have named our time together 'learning meetings,'" says principal Kim Bilanko of Ella Baker Elementary in Redmond, Washington. "Our agenda is predictable and aligned to our beliefs in building relationships and learning from each other. Each meeting includes the three Cs: connection, celebration, and collaboration. Each learning meeting also includes work-team time. Our staff is divided into four teams: Culture Club, Social Emotional Learning, Service-Learning, and Operations and Safety."

What if we began every faculty meeting by identifying three staff members who had gone above and beyond? Educators are remarkably shy about sharing their achievements, so a weekly e-mail could go out to everyone requesting nominations. I envision the principal or the chair of the School Spirit Committee announcing the names of three staff stars, reading selections from the nominating messages, awarding a candy bar or high-five, and leading the room in a round of applause.

In my *Education Week* article "What If Faculty Meetings Were Voluntary?" (2009b), I suggest beginning all meetings with an engaging question such as one of the following:

- "How can the administration help you become a better teacher?"
- "Who has been helpful to you in the past week?"
- "What is frustrating you?"
- "What curriculum should we deemphasize?"
- "What have you done in the past week that you'd do differently if you had the opportunity?"
- "What have you done in your classroom during the past week that makes you proud?"

In his book *Thinking, Fast and Slow* (2011), Daniel Kahneman notes that judges tend to offer more lenient parole to prisoners after lunch than they do in the morning—which suggests that having food at all meetings is a good idea if we want to keep people (relatively) happy. Kahneman also discusses the fact that we remember more vividly what happens most recently. This being the case, it's the end of the meeting, those last five minutes, that are likely to make the strongest impression on people. For this reason, it's a good idea to end meetings by saying things such as "Before we leave, let's spend a few minutes sharing what you learned here" or "Please share what was positive at the meeting" or

"What will you be doing tomorrow or next week because of what you heard today?" Ending meetings in this way can create and reinforce a powerful narrative. Make a point of being transparent and explaining your rationale so that participants can engage in the same practice when leading their own meetings.

An important part of a faculty or group pursuing SEL is knowing and trusting one another. A principal I know ends all faculty meetings by asking everyone to turn to their neighbor and tell them what they are looking forward to during the following week. This focus on positives and sharing with a colleague becomes part of the narrative that frames the culture.

Schoolwide Assemblies

Schoolwide assemblies present great opportunities to frame a narrative for everyone to hear. "We have Student of the Month assemblies," says Michelle Rooks of Jackson Hole Middle School in Wyoming. "Last year, we focused the awards on growth and improvement and a growth mindset. This year, we have created a kindness club. We are trying to increase awareness of what kindness looks and sounds like. We have just started something called the Kindness Shoutouts—kids can share kind acts they have witnessed. They also share kind acts from teachers and that they, themselves, have done. They share kindness they've seen in the media. It's been really cool to see what they consider kind." The school recently implemented Students' Choice Awards, in which students themselves choose the students of the month.

At Atkinson Academy in New Hampshire, the daily assembly starts with announcements, then students recite the Pledge of Allegiance and the Atkinson Academy Kindness Pledge: "I pledge to myself, on this very day, to try to be kind in every way. To every person, big or small. I will help them if they fall. When I love myself and others, too, that is the best that I can do." When I visited the school, 4th graders gave a presentation about what it means to be kind. The primary purpose of the assemblies is to continually teach and reinforce the CARES principles of challenge, acceptance, responsibility, empathy, and self-control.

Classrooms

In "How to Support the Emotional Link to Learning" (2018), Allison Posey discusses a Mood Meter, in which children identify their feelings with a color, character, or words:

- Positive/active (yellow, Elmo, happy and energized)
- Positive/de-active (green, Pooh bear, good and calm)
- Negative/active (red, Oscar the Grouch, bad and distressed)
- Negative/de-active (blue, Eeyore, bad and depressed)

For older students, consider identifying prominent fictional characters who embody these feelings rather than characters from *Sesame Street* and *Winnie the Pooh*.

At Essex Elementary in Massachusetts, "each class learns about the Mood Meter to determine how they are feeling at various times throughout the day and strategies to calm themselves down," says Roberts. "Students learn about taking a meta-moment to provide space between an emotion and a reaction."

In teaching students to set personal SEL goals and maintain focus, Laura Sweat, a 5th grade teacher at Grand Ridge Elementary in Washington, begins the year by asking students to think about the kind of adult that they hope to become and what it will require to do so. For example, she asks, "What do honest people do in situations where it could be tempting to cheat or lie? What do kind people do when they are paired with someone for a project that they don't necessarily like? What do hard-working people do when they don't understand something?" Her students envision scenarios and write descriptions about how they should act, then keep these goals and behavior expectations in binders and refer to them throughout the year.

Kim Nugent, instructional specialist at South Colby Elementary in Port Orchard, Washington, and colleague Steve Kaio-Maddox led implementation of the Formative Five at their school. They worked to ingrain awareness and understanding of the skills through many narratives. Kim says, "vocabulary and skills are an important part of our everyday life, with practice, practice, practice. We have songs for each skill (using old tunes and putting the specific skill to that tune), skill charts in each room and large anchor charts in the entry of our school. We have integrated it into our positive behavior systems, so that kids who are doing a great job of exhibiting a particular skill can wear a badge. It's been a great way for adults and kids from other classrooms to compliment them and ask what behavior or attitude earned them a badge."

Caryn Sawlis, behavior consultant for special populations at the Region 10 Education Service Center in Dallas, Texas, prepares educators to deal with stress, which includes sharing the difficulties she has personally experienced from overextending herself. Having been a first responder to a school shooting and following a tornado (along with many other traumas), she tells her audiences, she "suffered a nervous breakthrough a year ago. . . . I was working 60, 70 hours per week for months, no breaks . . . until I found myself on the floor screaming, 'I can't take this.'" Understandably, Sawlis's candor pulls the audience to her and opens educators up to thinking about their own lives. She continues, "Understanding behavior through the art of the story is all about relationships." Hearing this story would certainly lead others to reflect and think about what they might do to take care of themselves.

At Your School

- What's the narrative?
- What traditions do you have?
- What traditions should you create?

Place Survey

Before reading this chapter, please take a few minutes and respond to these survey items. An explanation and scoring system appear at the end of this survey.

Please indicate your perceptions by circling SA (strongly agree), A (agree), D (disagree), or SD (strongly disagree) by each item.

1. Signs and papers in the halls feature top-performing students.

    SA   A   D   SD

2. "We are safe" must be the only message on a school's exterior signs.

    SA   A   D   SD

3. We are bombarded with visual stimuli so blank walls in a school are comforting.

    SA   A   D   SD

4. A school's halls should educate.

    SA   A   D   SD

5. Furniture arrangement can be used to solve problems.

    SA   A   D   SD

6. What is posted in halls can affect adult morale and student learning.

    SA   A   D   SD

7. Displays in a hallway can be interactive and solicit input.

    SA   A   D   SD

8. Adults are most respectful and attentive when seated in well-organized rows.

    SA   A   D   SD

9. Encouraging students' parents to be at school longer than necessary is an invitation to crossed boundaries and difficulties.

    SA   A   D   SD

10. The time that people spend around coffee machines and copiers can foster congeniality and collegiality.

    SA   A   D   SD

11. If common spaces are to be decorated, this should be done by administrators.

    SA   A   D   SD

12. Classroom spaces should be designed and decorated by teachers.

    SA   A   D   SD

13. Students' restrooms should be clean and attractive and feature some decorations or art.

    SA   A   D   SD

14. Every child should be able to see his or her efforts on the walls.

SA   A   D   SD

15. Displays in a hallway can educate, entertain, and provoke.

SA   A   D   SD

The culture component surveys are designed to facilitate reflection and dialogue. After you have determined your score, I suggest that you answer the questions under item 1 below. Then, after two or three colleagues have also completed the survey, compare responses using the questions under item 2.

1. Does this score capture what happens in your school? Are there issues not addressed that you think are significant? Would your colleagues agree with your responses? If not, why might that be? Would your responses surprise colleagues?
2. On what items do you and your colleagues agree? When you disagree, why is that? Is there a correlation between how you see things and your position, years of experience, or another demographic factor? Were you previously aware of these different perceptions?

Scoring:

1. For items 4, 5, 6, 7, 10, 13, 14 and 15, give yourself 4 points for each SA and 3 points for each A. Subtract 4 points for each SD and 3 points for each D. Subtotal A= _____
2. For items 1, 2, 3, 8, 9, 11, and 12, give yourself 4 points for each SD and 3 points for each D. Subtract 4 points for each SA and 3 points for each A. Subtotal B= _____
3. Grand total (A + B) = _____

What Your Score Means:

- If your score is less than 30, your school needs to radically change how values are framed to support the place component.

- If your score is between 30–39, your school should review practices to see where improvements can be made in the place component.
- If your score is between 40–49, your school is doing a good job of supporting the place component, and you should look to see which area(s) need more attention.
- If your score is more than 50, your school is doing an excellent job of supporting the place component.

8

Place

Wherever we are, we are bombarded with messages. Whether we are walking in a park, shopping in a store, driving down the street, or eating dinner in our living room, messages surround us and tell us what is important and who we are. Some of these messages are intentional; advertisements and signs that tell us that we can define ourselves by what we eat, where we live, and how we use our time. Other messages stem from proximity to places and people—and though they are more subtle than intentional messages, they can also be far more powerful.

In schools, a cacophony of messages surrounds us at all times, even if we aren't aware of it. Cathy Davidson (2012) refers to our obliviousness in this respect as "attention blindness": "If things are habitual, we do not pay attention to them—until they become a problem" she writes (p. 49). Because a school is owned by both no one and everyone, the messages come from every direction in a range of volume, intensity, and relevance:

- Bake Sale Tomorrow
- No Firearms Allowed
- Go, Panthers, Go!
- Visitors Must Report to the Office

- 3rd Quarter Honor Roll Students
- No Food Past This Point!
- Every Child Succeeds at Bernard School

Entering a school, we are greeted by signs, slogans, banners, and metal detectors. Classroom walls are filled with student work, posters, grade expectations, and artifacts of personality and ownership. Most of these messages are intentionally sent through materials created or purchased to make a statement; others are unintentionally sent in the form of torn or dirty signage, cluttered or antiseptic settings, or a school entrance with unwelcoming bare walls. Alas, sometimes the unintentional messages are the most powerful.

If you are at school right now—or the next time you're there—take a few minutes to walk from just outside the front door of your school into the building, through the hall, and to the main office. As you do so, use the chart in Figure 8.1 to record what is visible. Don't limit your purview to formal signs.

One area not mentioned in the chart but that tells us a lot about a school's culture is the student restrooms. Rarely are these aesthetically pleasing spaces, and all too often they are not cleaned well or regularly enough. That's because in most schools, no one takes responsibility for the restrooms—except maybe the school custodian. What's the message to students when these areas are unclean, unsupervised, and unwelcoming? (To be fair, custodians are busy and often the condition of the student restrooms has not been made a high priority for them.) In my column "What Does Your Restroom Say About Your School?" (2015/2016), I share the following observations from administrators I had asked for insights on the topic:

- "Kids are unsupervised most of the time in the restroom."
- "Virtually every other minute [students are] in an adult's purview, but not in the restroom. Believe me, I know that because I wind up dealing with the aftermath."
- "Restrooms were rarely attractive and often not clean."

In the column, I note that things would be different if adults and students shared restrooms because the adults wouldn't accept dirty and unsanitary conditions. When was the last time you really looked at the student restrooms in your school? How might improving their appearance have a positive impact on school culture, student behavior, and faculty morale?

Perhaps no one appreciates the power of place more than an architect who creates learning environments in schools. Kevin Kerwin of HKW Architects, the designer of New City School's multiple intelligence library, is one such person, so I asked him to share his thinking. Here's what he had to say:

———————

The environment for me is a little like reading a book. There are whole chapters about culture, the organization and values present in every environment, and yes, what isn't said can be equally as important as what is said in the environment. The built environment is one of the best ways to understand people's values and motives, and this is made even more poignant in places that are mission driven. Openness and visibility within the environment support and promote communication.

Photos of the New City School library that Kerwin designed can be seen here: https://hkw.egnyte.com/fl/dyKMCVeVKa#folder-link/.

Given the power of place in our culture, it's surprising that more thought doesn't go into the images we face each day. Recently, for example, I visited some of my university students in two schools, one middle and one high school. The halls of the high school were filled with posters of previous graduating classes, signs heralding upcoming events, and student artwork. While I was there, students passed quietly and intently from class to class. At the middle school, however, the walls were almost barren, with few signs and no art, and student movement between classes was loud and chaotic. (My after-school meeting at the middle school was continually interrupted by loud, scratchy announcements over the intercom.) The high school halls said, "This is a place of

FIGURE 8.1
What's the Message?

	Welcome, inclusion	Security, safety	Student successes	Student progress
Outside the school				
In/by the main entrance				
In the halls				
In/by the main office				
Other common areas				

Explanations
- *Welcome, inclusion:* Beyond comfort and friendliness, is the school accessible to handicapped individuals? Is an embracing of a diversity of diversities obvious?
- *Security, safety:* Are signs clear about where to enter the building? Is the visitor sign-in sheet readily available and inviting? Are security personnel friendly and smiling?
- *Student successes:* Are student achievements visible in all intelligences (not just linguistic and logical-mathematical)? Do photographs capture students in gym class, dance, music, and sports? Is student art prominently displayed?
- *Student progress:* Are students' effort and progress reflected? Are values of empathy, self-control, integrity, embracing diversity, and grit shown? Do all kids have an opportunity to see themselves on the wall, not just those who are on the honor roll or sports teams?

Student activities	Upcoming events	Family engagement opportunities	Community events and opportunities	Faculty and staff highlights

- *Student activities:* What are students doing for fun? What clubs and teams are present? How are students contributing to the betterment of their school and community?
- *Upcoming events:* When are the future parent education sessions, school games or social times, parent organization or board of directors' meetings?
- *Family engagement opportunities:* What's available for parents and children to get involved?
- *Community events and opportunities:* What's happening in the larger community that might appeal to families and students?
- *Faculty and staff highlights:* Which teachers are featured this week or month? What teacher and administrator achievements (presentations, committee work, leadership roles, graduations, marriages, or family additions) can be shared? What other staff members are also celebrated?

Questions stemming from your observations are at the end of this chapter.

learning and we expect you to learn," whereas the middle school halls said, "You're on your own."

Schoolwide Strategies

Who is responsible for decorating and maintaining the common areas and shared spaces in a school? Lack of ownership for this responsibility is a major hurdle to ensuring that a place sends the messages we want. To raise a staff's awareness about the potential power of place, I suggest beginning by talking about the role of place as a part of organization culture, explain Davidson's "attention blindness," and then have each staff member walk through a portion of the building and complete the checklist in Figure 8.1. Afterward, convene everyone to talk about the messages that they did and didn't see. I have had my graduate school students do this in their schools, and we talk about their observations in class. They are often surprised at the messages they see and feel (it's also surprising how many of them visited areas in their buildings for the first time even though they were teaching there for years!).

Another option is to form a staff Ambient Learning Committee. This name reflects the fact that decorating spaces provides opportunities for the school to show what is important, to educate everyone, and to celebrate successes. The committee can assess what is present and what is missing in terms of school decor, and then determine what should be visible and who will be responsible for ensuring it, gathering input through the process (including from students). A productive way to begin this is to ask people to consciously look to see how retail establishments educate and sell through their décor and report what they learned to the committee.

Use the halls to inform *and elicit*. As part of our efforts to engage families and embrace diversity at New City School, we used Michele Norris' Race Card Project, an activity in which participants are asked to write six words on race. It's remarkable what insightful and candid thoughts these few words can inspire. We then placed staff members and upper-grade students' words on a hall bulletin board by the main office door and invited parents to contribute. We had blank 3" x 5" cards and a pen available so students' parents could also add their words. (More information on this project is available at www.theracecardproject.com.)

In his *Education Week* post "7 Simple Steps to Create a Positive School Climate," Peter DeWitt talks about the power of posters and pictures in the hall. He says, "Images matter. If they didn't, none of us would be on Facebook or Instagram. We gravitate to images because they evoke strong feelings inside. They remind us of simpler times or inspire us to step outside of our comfort zones" (2018). An example of this is at Yeatman-Liddell Middle School in St. Louis, Missouri, where a bulletin board outside the office features photos of staff members holding their favorite books.

The best way for people to learn is by being actively involved in creating knowledge. To this end, in learning about the power of place, teachers might distribute a floor plan of the school on an 8.5 x 11 inch sheet of paper and ask students to indicate areas of the building where they feel valued and safe by coloring them in green. They can also use red to identify areas where they feel unsafe or where they feel no attention is paid to their SEL. The colored-in floor plans can then be posted anonymously on the wall so that faculty members can review them and then discuss in small groups. Perception is reality, so we need to consider why students have marked an area red.

Signs in the halls at Timberlane Middle in New Hampshire encourage students to develop their SEL. At Atkinson Academy, one poster has the heading "Things We Can't Do *Yet*" and is filled with student writing. Another says, "Before you speak . . . THINK. T: Is it true? H: Is it helpful? I: Is it inspiring? N: Is it necessary? K: Is it kind?" A bulletin board titled "Empathy Is Putting Yourself in Someone Else's Shoes" has several shoes hanging from it, ensuring that it will be remembered. Another board is filled with student-made posters that give examples of how students are pursuing SEL skills. When I visited, the school was focusing on rigor, and the board showed examples of challenges that students are facing and for which they will need grit. (I appreciate their focus. When I present on the Formative Five, I always note that we should prioritize our efforts and not try to address all of them at once.)

The halls at Sandown Elementary have five "regulation stations," spaces and centers designed to let students stretch and use some extra energy when they are moving through the building. Assistant principal Christine Desrochers says, "We recognize that students need quick breaks from sitting, and they need to be able to move their bodies in order to be alert in class." Here's how Desrochers describes the five stations and their attendant directions:

- **Dancing Shoes:** "1. Start by standing on the blue piece of tape. 2. Look at the set of shoe prints in front of you. 3. Hop on the first set of shoe prints, making sure that your feet are facing the same direction as the shoe prints. 4. Continue hopping on the shoe prints, making sure to change your direction to match those of each print."

- **Strike a Pose:** "Yoga can help improve concentration and focus, strengthen posture and motor skills, and ease anxiety." Students are asked to take a yoga card and form the pose on it, then hold the pose while counting to 20. Students are encouraged to "take deep breaths while maintaining the position."

- **Hop to It! Hopscotch Move:** "1. Place your feet on the start square. 2. Hop to the next square. 3. As you finish, keep hopping to complete the movements."

- **Jumping Jacks:** Students are asked to do jumping jacks, elbow-to-knee touches, and windmills.

- **Get Calm:** "Deep breathing is an important part of helping our bodies relax, rejuvenate, and renew. When we take a deep breath, our body is telling our brain to slow down and relax." At this station, students are asked to relax—breathe in, breathe out—while tracing the lines of a five-pointed star. (This could be useful to staff, too!)

Students who guided me through the school were excited to be able to demonstrate the stations to me, and several times I saw kids walking in the hall who routinely veered off their paths to "do" a station. Desrochers says that these stations require students to practice the specific procedures with adults at the beginning of each school term.

At Fairway Elementary School in Missouri, principal Lorinda Krey seizes the spaces in her school's halls to form a culture that educates students, staff, and visitors about the Formative Five. For example, the entrance to the library just inside the school's front doors has a banner over it that says, "Fairway Elementary—Where we embrace grit, empathy, self-control, integrity, diversity." Next to the library door, a bulletin board titled "Who's Your Champion?" features photos of staff members holding signs with the names of their personal champions and a few sentences of explanation on them, many of which use the Formative Five terms. A bit further down the hall, a poster defines the Formative Five skills as follows using first-person terms generated by students:

- **Integrity:** I choose to do the right thing, even when no one is looking.
- **Empathy:** I understand and share what someone else is thinking and feeling.
- **Grit:** I step out of my comfort zone, risk failing, but I never give up.
- **Self-control:** I am in charge of my emotions, thoughts, words, and actions.
- **Embracing diversity:** I appreciate myself and celebrate the differences among all people.

The Formative Five skills are prominent when you enter South Colby Elementary in Port Orchard, Washington. Instructional specialist Kim Nugent expands: "We displayed a picture of our principal climbing a big mountain in the foyer for grit month, sticking a traffic light in his backpack for self-control month, and so on." A Formative Five bulletin board also greets those who enter the front door of Roosevelt School, with each skill accompanied by a photo of Roosevelt School students demonstrating it. Definitions followed by photos of students enacting the behaviors are also posted in classrooms: one asks, "What is self-control?" and features class photos showing well-behaved students sitting cross-legged on the floor. Another poster asks, "What can I do to help myself?" and shows photos of students sitting up, moving away, and raising their hands in class.

Walking through the halls of Villa Duchesne, a Roman Catholic high school in St. Louis, Missouri, I was struck by a series of large framed photos of groups of students, each portraying one of the school's five goals: a personal and active faith in God, respect for intellectual values, building community as a Christian value, social awareness that impels to action, and personal growth in an atmosphere of wise freedom. Each of the photos was a candid, un-posed photo of students engaged in activities reflecting the pursuit of these goals.

At Ella Baker School in Washington, the halls are filled with displays of "the Baker Eight" SEL traits and family photos. The school's principal, Kim Bilanko, says that families are asked to share photos of people who are important to them when they enroll their students. She adds, "We value the diverse backgrounds of students and are dedicated to having portraits of diverse leaders who have made a positive impact on our world."

Decorations can help to further a school's commitment to embracing diversity. "Many schools have pennants posted outside classrooms that reflect teachers' alma maters," says Omar Yanar of El Paso Leadership Academy in Texas, "and while we have those, we also intentionally feature schools that are further away, geographically and historically." For example, the school displays pennants from the Naval Academy in Annapolis and the University of California–Santa Barbara as well as a flag representing Seoul National University in Korea. According to Yanar, the school also has "'shout-out' bubbles on the front office television where positive statements from teacher to teacher, admin to teachers, and teachers to admin are posted on the TV. Student shout-outs coming soon!"

Christopher Truffer, regional assistant superintendent of the Arundel and South River clusters in Maryland's Anne Arundel Public Schools, notes that "each school has its own character, personality and 'feel.' . . . It becomes apparent in only a few minutes what the school community and staff value and hold dear. When you pass people in the hall, do they acknowledge you? Do people seem to be genuinely happy and appreciative, do they seem to enjoy the company of their colleagues, and especially, how do they interact with their students in a respectful, caring and nurturing manner?" He further notes that "Creating authentic dialogue connecting information and content to real-life experiences is a key to enhancing learning; where you see and hear this happening is where the most growth among students and adults is occurring."

At Arundel High, digital arts teacher Betsey Heeney had students form teams and create posters reflecting the Formative Five success skills. "My kids really embraced this project," said principal Davenport. "Not only did they learn about the Formative Five, I think they really nailed the essences in a graphic format. My print and design shop are enlarging the posters and mounting them for display in my building." (I am also including them in my presentations on the Formative Five.)

Classroom Strategies

Typically, classrooms display posters or photos that speak to the curriculum being taught. Depending on the grade and class, walls and cabinet doors are covered with pictures of animals, maps, photos of prominent people, drawings of historical characters, sunrises and sunsets, the periodic table of elements, graphs, or perfect or near-perfect papers. Even when these items are attractively arrayed, the effect is a bit like white noise—numbing. Maps are different than photos of prominent people, and no one will confuse a graph with a picture of dogs, but there's a sameness because of what *isn't* there: too often, these displays are for students, but not *of* them.

All children should see themselves—their efforts and progress—on the walls; even if they aren't there today, they must feel like they could be there tomorrow. Those perfect and near-perfect papers leave out 80 percent of students (as does the highly attractive art in the halls). It's not surprising that many classrooms lack personalization given the generic quality of so many other spaces around us: "Everything about the modern office building was designed to signal that this is not your home; this is not fun; this is not personal; this is not about *you*" (Davidson, 2012, p. 183).

That what we see connotes value and legitimacy is the focal point in a lesson taught by Chris Hass, a 2nd and 3rd grade teacher in Richland School District 2, South Carolina. He worked from a book, *Milo's Museum* (written by Zetta Elliott), in which a young black girl visits a museum with her class and notes with discomfort that none of her culture's artifacts are present. After she talks with her grandfather and aunt and learns about the role of curator, she creates a museum for her backyard. As her peers visit, they bring artifacts so that the museum reflects the community. After his class read the book, Hass says:

The questions my kids generated included a few about the injustice of such practices—museums not adequately representing those in our communities. Two of the girls in class asked if we could make our own class museum and bring things from our homes to put in it. I gladly urged them to start planning how this might work. Soon, they created a sign, set aside spaces in the room for the artifacts, and invited everyone to bring stuff in. We wound up with photos, medals, trophies, art work, mementos, jerseys, rock collections, and so on. It was a great experience for all of us (certainly me!) to learn the power of making our classroom a space that explicitly shows our appreciation and love for one another while also working in deliberate ways to better know the home lives of our friends and classmates.

Posting photos of your students in the classroom is a wonderful way to support SEL skills. These could be individual photos, a class or school group photo, or family photos (however students define family). Differences within, between, and among photos can help support empathy and diversity and, depending on what activity is being shown, grit. Keeping up photos of students from previous classes also sends a message to everyone that positive relationships transcend the classrooms in which students learn in a given year. (Additional examples of ways to reinforce SEL skills along the classroom walls can be seen in Figure 8.2.)

In "Spreading Social-Emotional Learning Across All Schools" (2018), Evie Blad describes how furniture and practice can be designed to help students. "At Jason Lee Middle School, for example, teachers can send students to a 'reset desk' in each classroom to reflect on how their behavior affected classmates," she writes. "Students can also send themselves to the reset desk to take a break before re-entering the classroom conversation" (p. 9).

Similarly, at New City School, we designated seating areas in classrooms and on the playground as places where students could gather to solve disagreements. Chris Wallach, a New City School 1st grade teacher, explains: "We had the red chairs in our classroom where students could resolve conflicts. If someone asked you to go there, you did. This year, I had two peace chairs in my room. We use the responsive classroom idea of having a 'take a break' place where kids can go on their own or be asked to go to consider how they might redirect themselves." A former New City 4th grade teacher, Carla Duncan, adds: "I called the red chairs my 'discussion place' because I had painted the seats red. I most often

FIGURE 8.2	
SEL on the Walls	
Formative Five Success Skill	**Examples That Teach and Reinforce SEL**
Empathy	• Definitions of the three levels of empathy (see p. 30) with student photos illustrating each one • Images of people who see things from a different perspective than students do, with possible explanations why that is (Menzel and Mann's book *A Material World: A Global Family Portrait* is a good resource) • Evidence—photos, articles, notes—from altruistic individual or class projects
Self-control	• A poster of students' personal goals and class goals • Bar graphs showing students' reflections on their progress • A running total of the number of days without an altercation or when all homework was submitted
Integrity	• Current photos and accounts of leaders who took a tough stand even though it cost them • A graph for students to check their name when they showed integrity by interrupting bullying or an unfair comment • A chart to record the number of times when integrity was discussed outside of school
Embracing Diversity	• Photos and 3 x 5 cards of when students and families left their comfort zones to talk to people who were different than them • Student-generated Michele Norris Race Cards and a separate display of those collected from family members • Bar graphs from student interviews of grandparents showing how the world has (and has not) changed from when they were the students' age
Grit	• Examples of "doing better" or a positive trajectory • Photos of projects that evince lots of grit with accompanying explanations • Photos of students using grit in non-school settings

referred to them as 'problem-solving chairs.' The rules were simple: If a student had a problem with someone, he or she could invite that person to meet at the chairs. I never sent someone to the chairs. I may have suggested to a student that the chairs were available for their use if they seemed to have forgotten. The chairs were most used after recess; for some children if recess problems are not handled in a timely manner, they might not be able to focus for the time after it."

Additional Factors Related to Space

Place includes aspects that we may not typically consider, such as lighting. In "How a Room's Lighting Shapes Our Decisions" (2018), Emily Ayshford shows how dimly lit spaces encourage people to be a bit less conventional and restrained than they otherwise would be and make more pleasurable choices (e.g., ordering desserts). "We feel less connected to others in the dark," writes the author. "So, we assign less weight to what others think and more weight to what we authentically desire." Thus, if you want folks to feel a bit creative, you might want to dim the lights. If you do this, I suggest explaining your rationale to further encourage adventurous thinking and remind everyone that place matters.

There is merit in gathering in designated meeting spaces, but I recommend holding faculty meetings in classrooms and starting them with the host teacher explaining his or her purposeful, SEL-related decoration choices to the others. It's amazing how often teachers have not been in each other's classrooms despite working in the same building for years.

Where we sit and how we position ourselves is an important consideration in determining how effective a meeting will be. At faculty meetings, teachers tend to sit next to colleagues from the same department or grade—those with whom they work closest. That's understandable, but close working relationships can inhibit when schoolwide issues are being addressed. The pressure to go along with your teammates can be quite powerful. To avoid this obstacle, have everyone count off by a number to establish groups of three or four when large-scale issues are discussed. Interacting with different colleagues than usual also helps build a feeling of collegiality.

We should also consider occasionally departing radically from our customary seating arrangement. Doorley and Witthoft (2012) suggest sitting in a circle, as though gathered around a campfire: "The 'camp-fire' configuration can dramatically impact the quality of an activity. In the absence of actual flames, the posture and arrangement of people sitting around a fire (sitting low to the ground in a tight circle) heightens the awareness of group participants and the activity topic" (p. 32). I wouldn't sit this way regularly—the novelty adds to the power—but I can envision it helping people make connections with one another and think more creatively.

Steve Jobs was noted for designing workspaces to force interaction. Walter Isaacson (2014) writes: "When Steve Jobs designed a new headquarters for Pixar, he obsessed over ways to structure the atrium, and even where to locate the bathrooms, so that serendipitous personal encounters would occur. Among his last creations was the plan for Apple's new signature headquarters, a circle with rings of open workspaces surrounding a central courtyard." Similarly, in *The Culture Code*, Coyle says, "What mattered most in creating a successful team had less to do with intelligence and experience and more to do with where the desks happened to be located" (2018, p. 70). He recommends "Create spaces that maximize collisions" (p. 82).

As we think about how to create collaborative spaces, we need to remember that not everyone is an extrovert. In her 2012 book *Quiet*, Susan Cain writes: "If you're a manager, remember that one-third to one-half of your workforce is probably introverted, whether they appear that way or not. Think twice about how you design your organization's office space. Don't expect introverts to get jazzed up about open office plans or, for that matter, lunchtime birthday parties or team-building retreats. Make the most of introverts' strengths—these are people who can help you think deeply, strategize, solve complex problems, and spot canaries in your coal mine" (p. 265).

At New City School, we had a small parent area set up across from the main office in the front hall that featured a couch, two big easy chairs, a rug, a box of infant toys, and a coffee pot under a sign that read, "Parents, have a cup of coffee. Linger with us." That space was often filled with four or five parents in the morning after they dropped off their children, and again in the afternoon prior to pick-up (rarely were the same parents there at both times). Beyond providing a comfortable waiting and chatting space for these parents, the visibility of the space and the welcoming sign sent a loud and clear message to parents: We are on the same team!

Because going to the principal's office can be nerve-wracking to many, we should strive to make this space as positive and welcoming as possible. Katharine Schwab (2019) writes about "biophilic design" being "the idea that incorporating natural elements will make people feel more comfortable in spaces." She describes a doctor's office filled with plants, comfortable couches, and tables that make it seem like a coworking space. The goal of the design is "to ease patients' nerves and show them that going to the doctor doesn't have to be a negative experience." Having plants and comfortable seating is a good beginning, but it is only a start. Administrative spaces, just like classroom spaces, need to feature student work, signs of positive student trajectory, and SEL skills.

The power of place is evident in Michelle Obama's comments about her husband's need for a certain kind of space. "Barack, I've come to understand, is the sort of a person who needs a hole, a closed-off little warren where he can read and write undisturbed," she writes in her memoir *Becoming* (2018). "It's like a hatch that opens directly onto the spacious skies of his brain. Time spent there seems to fuel him. In deference to this, we've managed to create some version of a hole inside every home we've lived in—any quiet corner or alcove will do. . . . For him, the hole is a kind of sacred high place, where insights are birthed and clarity comes to visit. For me, it's an off-putting and disorderly mess" (p. 181).

If Elephants Can Do It . . .

Too often, principals and teachers become accustomed to their surroundings and setting and miss opportunities to use place to support values and SEL. "Environments can be used not just to represent cultural values but also to inspire them," write Doorley and Witthoft in *Make Space: How to Set the Stage for Creative Collaboration* (2012, p. 22). We need to be aware of the power of place in determining culture and framing behavior, especially the importance of SEL in a school. We can take guidance from animals, birds who fashion nests from twigs and debris, and dogs who circle to flatten the grass before lying down. Intuitively, they know that they need to modify the environment to fit their needs. Consider the following example that comes from the jungle:

The environment shapes every species that inhabits it. As species struggle to survive, they evolve adaptations to their surroundings, whether they're fish gaining antifreeze in the Arctic Ocean, or hummingbirds evolving oxygen-hungry blood for flying over the Andes. But some species can reverse the equation. Even as the environment shapes them, they shape the environment. Elephants, for example, tear down tree branches and split their trunks down the center. Lizards, insects, and other animals can then invade the trees, which were previously off-limits to them. The rampages of the elephants open light into dense forests, allowing small plants to sprout up, providing food to animals like gorillas and bush pigs. Elephants can convert open woodlands into savannas and keep them cleared and fertilized with their dung. The elephants thus live in a habitat of their own making. (Zimmer, 2018, p. 467)

Look at the chart in Figure 8.1 again—bearing in mind that no school can fully address each of the listed categories—and ask yourself whether the messages you see are those that you want your school to be sending. Is there any category for which no indicators are present at your school? Were you surprised at the number of messages? What do the walls and halls say about your school's culture? We should view these spaces as opportunities for ambient learning and seize them as ways to deliver our SEL messages.

At Your School

- Is the value of SEL apparent in your halls and classrooms?
- What new signage, seating, and lighting could develop SEL?
- What current aspects of place need to change to support SEL?

9

Leadership Musings

Though I wrote this chapter with administrators in mind, the strategies here can be initiated by anyone regardless of title, and, in fact, are most likely to succeed if everyone responsible for implementing them has some background knowledge about them. Any SEL implementation should be characterized by intentionality and transparency: We should be thoughtful and deliberate about what we hope to do, and we should share our plans and rationale with others in our school community. Doing this is a sign of respect and trust for the people with whom we work and increases the likelihood that new ideas will be accepted. Intentionality and transparency are worth pursuing in any sphere of school administration, from implementing a new math curriculum to changing how sick days are accumulated, and only more so when it comes to issues that focus on emotions and relationships. We must use our SEL if we want to develop others' SEL.

Make the Case

Our students need SEL to become successful adults—period. As I noted earlier, their scholastic success should be the floor, not the ceiling. This is not a surprise to educators. Schools are tiny microcosms of society—collections of people, interactions, and relationships—so we see students in many different situations. We see them working on tasks that are easy and hard. We see them in groups, we observe them when they are frustrated, we notice how they respond when confronted with difficult choices, and we are aware of what they do when they interact with others who are different than they are. We also see them when they are alone. We understand which student's SEL skills propels him forward or gives her an advantage; we also know how weak SEL skills affect everything that a student touches. That awareness is why you are reading this book and why ASCD embraces the whole child.

Unfortunately, many parents aren't aware of how important it is for their children to develop SEL skills at schools. An important part of our job, then, is to make the case for SEL to them. On a regular basis, they need to see that SEL *works*. Here are some helpful data in support of SEL that you can share with parents:

- In *The Impact of Enhancing Students' Social and Emotional Learning: A Meta-Analysis of School-Based Universal Intentions* (Durlak, Weissberg, Dymnicki, Taylor, & Schellinger, 2011), the authors present findings from 213 school-based, universal social and emotional learning (SEL) programs involving 270,034 kindergarten through high school students. They found that SEL participants demonstrated significantly improved social and emotional skills, attitudes, behavior, and academic performance that reflected an 11-percentile-point gain in achievement" (p. 1).

- In *From A Nation at Risk to a Nation At Hope* (Aspen Institute, 2019), the authors cite:
  - "An analysis of more than 200 studies of programs that teach students social and emotional skills found that these efforts significantly improved student behavior, feelings about school, and most importantly achievement, and made schools safer" (p. 7).
  - "Eight in 10 employers say social and emotional skills are the most important to success and yet are also the hardest skills to find" (p. 14).

— "Research reveals that teachers' own social and emotional competencies influence the quality of the learning experiences they offer their students. In addition, a growing body of research suggests that developing teachers' social and emotional competencies improves teacher well-being, reduces stress and burnout, and can reduce teacher and principal turnover. Teachers also report greater job satisfaction when their students are more engaged and successful" (p. 25).

- In his 2018 *EdSurge* article "The Future of Education Depends on Social Emotional Learning: Here's Why," Giancarlo Brotto reports on an OECD (Organization for Economic Co-operation and Development) study that "revealed a lack of SEL regularly correlated with unfavorable outcomes such as an increased chance of unemployment, divorce, poor health, criminal behavior and imprisonment."

- From "These Are the Skills That Your Kids Will Need for the Future (Hint: It's Not Coding)," Greg Satell (2018) notes that "The high-value work today is being done in teams and that will only increase as more jobs become automated. The jobs of the future will not depend as much on knowing facts or crunching numbers, but will involve humans collaborating with other humans to design work for machines. Collaboration will increasingly be a competitive advantage."

Be sure to share this kind of information regularly with the school community. Every weekly parent letter and school newsletter should contain some data about SEL and an example of an activity at school that advances the Formative Five. The same is true of faculty bulletins and faculty meetings. The Three *T*s rule for effective communication applies: Tell them what you are going to tell them, tell them, and then tell them what you told them. Repetition not only increases the likelihood that others will hear and absorb the message, it indicates how important that message is.

Here's how Craig Hinkle, principal of Richland Collegiate High School in Dallas, Texas, uses SEL skills to talk with the parents of prospective students:

_____

I'm going to talk about me, my educational background, my struggles, and me as a teacher. I think it's important that you understand where I'm coming from so you know where we are going as a school. I failed out of college the first time. Yes, the principal of a collegiate program just admitted to you that he failed out of college. You are wondering if I'm the best person for this job? I think that is precisely what makes me perfect for this job. I know the pitfalls, I know how it feels, and I know how to recover from the failure.

_____

I graduated in the top 10 percent from my high school and was accepted to Texas A&M. Within three semesters, I had an astounding 1.3 GPA. When I called my dad, he sighed and asked, "Son, did you try?" "Dad," I said, "I've never tried harder at anything in my life." "Then it was a good failure," he replied.

_____

At my school, we don't just celebrate successes—we acknowledge failures, too. Failures are about learning. In fact, good failures can sometime teach you more than passing everything and having a high GPA. While our program is extremely rigorous, while we add an ungodly amount of work for the high school students to do, they come in knowing immediately that even their principal has failed miserably. They also know that while we don't celebrate failure, we aren't going to falsely give you anything. Everything must be earned, it is hard, and ultimately, we are here to help you learn how to learn.

Principal Janine Gorrell of North Side Community School in Missouri used Back to School Night to address students' academic and social-emotional needs with parents. She organized the presence of a few local social service providers at the school so that families could easily visit with them in the gym after they had visited their children's classrooms. Among the providers were groups providing low-income or free housing information, free uniforms and school attire, free medical and health support, support for fathers, counseling, and free extracurricular activities. Throughout the year, Gorrell continues inviting families to school for ongoing parent meetings, family engagements, and special family events.

I often used the beginning of our Back to School Night at New City School to proselytize for SEL. One year, I distributed blank notecards and pens to parents as they entered the school theater to meet me before going to their children's classrooms (you can imagine the querulous looks that elicited). After welcoming all the parents and introducing the teachers, I said, "I'll bet you're wondering why you were given a blank card and pen. Relax, it's not a test! What I want you to do is write the initials of three people you know personally whom you consider to be successful. How you define that success is up to you."

After waiting a couple of minutes for parents to write their responses, I asked them to turn and form groups of four or five in which to share their reasons for their choices. "My concern isn't who," I said, "and I don't want you to share names. What I want you to discuss is what caused you to name someone. What were the characteristics that you identified? Are these the qualities that you want to see in your children?" After folks had exchanged their ideas, I asked for people to share if there had been any characteristics noted by more than one person in their small group.

Over the years, I did this exercise a few times and the result always turned out the same. When parents identified the characteristics of people who were successful, they cited the ability to work well with others and be kind and caring; to be responsible and honest; to show focus and grit; to partner well with others; and to be confident. They enthusiastically said they hoped their children would have these qualities. Of course, they were sharing how much they valued SEL even though they didn't use the term (in those days, we called SEL skills the "personal intelligences"). I ended by telling them they had described exactly the qualities that we were working to develop in their children. Our students' parents then went to their children's classrooms feeling confident about our SEL focus and appreciating our efforts.

As good a start as this was, I knew that it wasn't enough. Throughout the year I used my weekly letters and parent education evenings, along with displays in the halls, to share the importance of SEL in preparing students to succeed in life. Sometimes I included an article or a quote about the importance of SEL; occasionally I wrote about a child or an adult who gained attention for exhibiting these qualities; often I shared what we were doing to develop SEL at school and why it was important to prepare children to succeed in life. Intentionality and transparency framed all my communications about SEL.

It's essential that we solicit feedback, so every year I included a reference to SEL in my spring parent survey by asking parents to respond to strongly agree, agree, disagree, or strongly disagree with the following statement: "New City has a strong commitment to moral values and character development." Results were always gratifying, but honestly, we were not as good as parents thought we were. In my last year at the school, 42 percent of families returned the survey, and 98 percent of them strongly agreed or agreed with the statement. Their satisfaction was evidence that they valued SEL and were pleased with the growth they saw in their children. Of course, I was bothered by the 2 percent.

Drop Your Tools!

Twenty-seven wildland firefighters tragically died in two forest fires 45 years and hundreds of miles apart: at Mann Gulch, Montana, in 1949, and at South Canyon, Colorado, in 1994. In both situations, fires that were thought to be manageable roared out of control, engulfing the firefighters and ending their lives. Many, perhaps all, of those deaths could have been avoided.

How are these tragic deaths relevant to SEL? Because change is never easy, even if everyone wants it. Many of the firefighters died because they were unwilling, maybe unable, to follow the command, "Drop your tools!" and run. Laden in heavy protective gear and carrying 45 pounds of equipment, their bodies were found clutching their tools—chainsaws and axes—and wearing their packs. The men were outraced and killed by the rapidly advancing flames—30 feet high and traveling as fast as 660 feet per minute—while carrying equipment that they could have discarded (Weick, 1996a). From our perspective, dropping them seems wise, but the tools were part of the firefighters' identities; this equipment was *part* of being a forest firefighter. So when the situation quickly changed and carrying equipment became a dangerous liability, the men could not respond.

In "Drop Your Tools: An Allegory for Organizational Studies" (1996b), Karl E. Weick notes that giving up tools may feel like giving up control and that "to drop one's tools may be to admit failure." For teachers and principals, the tools that are so hard to discard include the 3 *Rs*, standardized achievement tests, letter grades, and textbook-driven lessons. Many educators rail against these tools, but they have been forced to use them for so long that changing practices is very difficult. As intimidating as it can be to try something new and uncomfortable, it may be even more daunting to set aside what is familiar. Changing curriculum and trying new pedagogical approaches are not life and death issues, but they can elicit anxiety, fear, and resistance, nonetheless. In *Seven Secrets of a Savvy School Leader* (2010), Rob Evans notes that even when change is proclaimed as a positive and forward movement, people's reactions are often quite different. "Growth and development may be the ideal synonyms for change, but grief and bereavement are every bit as accurate," he writes. "We are often reluctant to abandon patterns even when we dislike them" (p. 43).

We know that old habits die hard and that ignoring or glossing over the need for SEL is an old habit. Unfortunately, as Yuval Noah Harari (2017) writes, "Knowledge that does not change behavior is useless." It's not enough to understand the value of the Formative Five; we need to create momentum for teaching SEL skills to students and developing them ourselves, and we must appreciate the power of allies in creating momentum.

We need to begin by convening a few people—fewer than 10—who understand the value of the Formative Five; from that initial group, we engage and persuade, adding and expanding. John Tedesco, CEO of the e-commerce customer relationship management platform Drip, describes this concentric model of change in a 2017 LinkedIn post: "Rather than a broadcast or 'boil the ocean' approach to modifying organizational behavior, the CEO or department head should start with a small group of either her direct reports or key influencers. This could be the executive leadership team for a CEO or a group of principal engineers for an engineering organization." An attractive aspect of the concentric approach to change is that it need not begin at the top of the organization. It's certainly easier when official leaders lead, but a remarkable amount of energy can be created by a small nucleus of people, regardless of their role or hierarchical position, and then expanded.

After a group has taken root, create a plan for implementing an SEL orientation by answering the following question: "How can we advance the Formative Five through our values and mission, practices, people, narrative, and place?" Discussing this question in depth offers opportunities to promote faculty collegiality while honing our skills. As mentioned earlier in this book, it's valuable for people to have opportunities to fashion their own solutions and construct personal knowledge for themselves—what Jeremy Heimans and Henry Timms refer to as "the IKEA effect"—"A tendency of people to place a higher value on self-made products" (2018, p. 126). They note that if an idea "feels 'untouchable' or overly polished, it is very hard for others to feel they can take the reins and make it their own" (p. 46). A public process also creates accountability for all concerned.

Connect, Engage, and Model

Leadership is ultimately about relationships. It's simple but it's true. We follow others because of the confidence and trust we have in them; their title and position matter far less than our relationship with them. We may not even know them personally, but we have enough knowledge to have a relationship of confidence. The most effective leaders connect, engage, and model the behaviors they espouse. Their leadership stems not from hierarchy or a podium, but because of the relationships they have developed. They have built upon their empathy, what Chung calls "the path for exchanging values within our communities and with others" (2016, p. 72) to earn the trust and respect of others.

"This may seem like a no-brainer," notes Katie Morgan in "A Guide to Changing Someone Else's Beliefs: Use the Science of Persuasion to Your Advantage" (2019), "but it's much easier to influence people who are already close to you." She then quotes Robert Cialdini: "Most of us think that the message and the merits of the message are the things that will convince people. . . . That's usually not the case. Very often, it's the relationship we have to the messenger. It's not always about the argument, but about the delivery." Henry Cloud notes that the most successful messages are reciprocated: "True listening and understanding only occurs when the other person understands that you understand (2009, p. 60).

Leaders listen and respond to others. They also need to share about themselves to let their colleagues know them, too. Leaders need to be open about their goals, plans, and satisfactions. They also should share their fears and frustrations. Opening the dialogue in this way builds relationships that enable everyone to grow together. Just as in every other aspect of building, maintaining, and advancing a relationship, frequent and trusting communications are essential.

Relationships don't grow and prosper without attention and care. It's easy to take them for granted and assume that they will stay strong, but that's not something anyone can assume. Relationships aren't static; they either wither or strengthen. "Don't take relationships for granted," observes Michael Fullan. "The engaged principal is always building and tending to relationships" (2014, p. 135). To maintain strong relationships, we must focus on the positive. The 5:1 approach—give others five positive comments to every negative—advocated by psychologist John Gottman can be a very effective tool in this regard. In my column for *Educational Leadership* (2009a), I likened this approach to a checking account: "Your 'deposits'—positive comments or interactions—must remain greater than your withdrawals," I wrote. "A one-to-one ratio of positives to negatives is deadly and makes it likely that well-intentioned critical comments will fall on deaf ears. A three-to-one ratio is an improvement, but it probably won't move the relationship forward."

Sometimes a question is heard as negative even if that wasn't the intent. For example, after conducting classroom walkthroughs as a principal, I was sometimes aware that my simple information-seeking questions were perceived as criticisms. "What was happening with the two boys in the back of the room?" was heard as "Why didn't you have those two boys participating with the rest of the class?"; "What were you trying to accomplish?" as "Your lesson was really unclear." This underscores the importance of listening, learning what others heard, and not simply assuming that your intent was clearly taken. A neutral remark or simply not saying anything can also be perceived as a negative. Praise should be valid and specific: saying "Nice job" may elicit a smile but it's nowhere near as effective as "You did a nice job of responding to that student's question."

Social-emotional learning relies heavily on building healthy relationships among students, between students and teachers, and among all staff members. Invariably, a staff that pursues SEL and implements the Formative Five will take risks together and come to respect and care for one another in a meaningful way. Their interactions will become more positive and trusting as they work to develop these same qualities in their students. It's understandable if school bus drivers, security personnel, cafeteria workers, and lunchroom aides cannot attend all PD activities or faculty meetings, but they should be informed, involved, and engaged as much as possible.

An important part of the role of administrators is to step back and observe what people are doing, how funds are being spent, what information is posted on school walls, and how we know our students are progressing. This purview is especially important in implementing SEL because we don't have standardized tests to record our progress (thankfully) and too often thinking about SEL and the Formative Five can be pushed aside in the hustle to cover traditional curriculum. Thus, administrators need to be sure that SEL is a priority, that it's pursued in classrooms and faculty meetings, that it's evident on halls and walls, and that it is a regular part of the educator-student-parent dialogue.

Social-emotional learning "is for every adult and every kid, all day every day. Attending to emotions is necessary on the bus, in the playground, in the cafeteria, after school, and during academic classes," writes Joshua P. Starr (2019). "Every adult has a role to play in creating a consistent and emotionally healthy school climate, rather than leaving it to the social worker or the school psychologist or a handful of popular teachers."

At Your School

- How can leaders make the case for SEL?
- How can leaders support SEL efforts?
- How can leaders widen the SEL leadership circle?

10

Conclusion

The older I become, the more uncertainties I face. In my younger years, much seemed sure and logical. Now, though, I question many things:

- How would the United States be different if the first settlers had arrived from Asia on the shores of San Diego in 1620 instead of Plymouth Rock? What if the writings of Confucius had framed American society rather than the Magna Carta?

- How different would American society be today if every adult 21 years of age or older had been given the right to vote in 1789? What laws would have been passed, how soon would slavery have been abolished, and what wars would have been avoided?

- How will we respond when life on other worlds is discovered? Will it make any difference if that life is thousands of light years away and there is no real contact?

- How can it be that there's a designated hitter in baseball's American League but pitchers must bat in the National League?

Although these questions don't keep me awake at night, they do take up more space in my brain than they should; after all, there's not much that I can do about them. There are, however, three core beliefs that I know, from experience, to be true:

169

- Teachers are the most important factor in determining a child's success and the quality of a school, and a school's culture can enhance the work of teachers and increase the effectiveness of administrators.
- The job of principals is to work with teachers to create a culture of trust and growth. A school's culture is forged by principals and teachers working collaboratively.
- Educators must prepare students to succeed in life, not just to do well in school. A school's culture must embrace SEL and the Formative Five.

These three beliefs are reflected in the pages of this book.

The kinds of educators who make a difference for students are those who are filled with high aspirations, audacious goals, and never-completed checklists. They never get as far as they would like, perform as well as they hoped, or run out of things to do. I love to hire these kinds of people! But I also know that I will worry about them, occasionally have to ask them to slow down, offer consolation when that perfect plan goes awry, and try to help them not be so hard on themselves. It is very likely that educators who are developing the Formative Five and implementing SEL will experience some failures and frustrations and become self-critical. Although we should all have high goals and do our best, we need to be realistic and take care of ourselves.

This message was brought home to me years ago at a principals' conference. Speaking at a conference on how administrators can handle stress, a principal began by relaying how important he felt it was to have all his students put away their cafeteria trays. There were some guffaws in the audience and he reacted with indignation, explaining that his students were mostly wealthy and white, while the cafeteria workers were generally women of color in low-paying jobs. "These kids shouldn't feel that the staff needs to pick up after them," the principal told the now-chagrined crowd. "Now," he said, "more than 95 percent of the students now put away their trays. That's not everyone," he said, "But I've learned that when I push for that 100 percent, the cafeteria feels like a prison, I make everyone around me crazy, and my stress level goes through the ceiling. I've learned to settle for excellence and not pursue perfection."

I sat in the audience and thought about areas where I was chasing perfection instead of settling for excellence. Several situations came to mind where teachers were making good progress but weren't yet where I wanted them to be; I needed, I now knew, to step back and be realistic about what I could expect of them. I also reflected that I had not been getting into classrooms as much as I liked, despite it being a priority. I observed newer teachers and those who were struggling on a regular basis, but I was not as successful as I wanted to be in visiting my senior teachers, those who had the ship running smoothly. They still wanted me to visit, and I wanted to be there, so I was frustrated at my inability to make the time to do so. (Please pause for a minute or two and think of where this excellence versus perfection might apply to you and your job. I would be surprised if you don't have at least a couple of examples.)

Excellence versus perfection: It's an easy concept to understand but a difficult one to enact, particularly for the Type A educators who make a difference in schools. But settling for excellence does not mean accepting mediocrity, only that we must prioritize our time and energies and be fair to ourselves about what is realistic. It's easy to assume that we need not be hindered or slowed by the obstacles we will inevitably face in our work. That's a mistake. Whatever your role, working in a school is a marathon, not a sprint, and we need to take care of our ourselves so that we can tend to others.

I hope that this book has been helpful to you. We are on the same team, so please contact me at trhoerr@newcityschool.org or trhoerr@ aol.com if there's anything I can do to help.

Acknowledgments

Writing this book has been a wonderful experience. I have been in contact with many wise, caring, and generous people, and I have learned from them. I've visited schools, read books and articles, attended conferences, and engaged in affirming and disquieting conversations about education, school leadership, social-emotional learning, character development, The Formative Five, and life. It has been fun!

But the writing has also been humbling and painful at times. This comes from the fact that writing about what should happen in schools reminds me all too well of what I didn't do and what I could have done better. I recognize that this thinking leads me down the "excellence versus perfection" rabbit-hole, but it does make me wish I could hop in a time-machine and have a do-over. I'd so love the opportunity to do a better job of practicing what I preach. David Brooks captures this tension well in *The Second Mountain: The Quest for a Moral Life*, when he says, "We try to teach what it is that we really need to learn" (2019, p. xx). I hope that this book can provide to others some of the guidance and help that I sorely needed.

I have spent far more time engaged in research for this book than I ever anticipated. Similar to how I felt when I was working on my doctoral dissertation, it has been hard for me to say "enough is enough"; there is always another article begging to be read. And the ease of jumping from article to article on the internet has made that temptation much harder to resist. If it's possible to over-read (and I'm not sure that it is), I plead guilty as I glance up from my book!

My name is on the cover of this book and my computer's keys are worn from the millions—literally—of keystrokes that created the text, but this book could not have been written without the good ideas and support that I received from many, many talented and caring people. In wanting to learn how other educators were addressing SEL and implementing the Formative Five, I sent hundreds of e-mails, had numerous phone calls, visited schools, and consumed more caffeine at local meeting places than was good for my sleep. In every interaction, people willingly gave their time and shared their ideas. Truly, I am indebted to each of these people for so willingly taking the time and sharing their thoughts.

I begin with offering appreciation to the many helpful and friendly educators at the schools I visited in Iowa, Maryland, Missouri, New Hampshire, and Tennessee, especially the people who kindly invited me, escorted me, and took care of the logistics. My gracious hosts were Brett Abbotts, the principal of Roosevelt Elementary in Iowa; Gina Davenport, the principal of Arundel High in Maryland; Julie Frugo, the head of the Premier Charter School in Missouri; Lorinda Krey, the principal of Fairway Elementary School in the Rockwood School District, Missouri; Patrice Lift, the assistant principal/curriculum coordinator at Atkinson Academy in the Timberlane Regional School District, New Hampshire; and Thor Kvande, the head of the Grace-St. Luke's School in Tennessee. Special thanks also goes to Kim Bilanko, the principal of Ella Baker School in Washington, and Omar Yanar, the CEO of El Paso Leadership Academy in Texas, because while I have not visited them (yet), they were so incredibly gracious in their e-mails and phone calls that I feel as if I have been at their schools. Each visit, real or virtual, was a tremendous learning opportunity for me, and I cannot thank these folks enough.

I am also indebted to so many people who shared ideas and articles, chatted with me, gave me feedback, pushed my thinking, and served as inspirational role models by embodying learning and sharing. Deep thanks go to the following people: Andy Abbott, Barry Anderson, Carla Anderson-

Diekmann, Kristi Arbetter, Nancy Barcelos, Michael Barolak, Marvin Berkowitz, Sheldon Berman, Mindy Bier, Mary Biggs, Stephanie Bowman, the guys in my book group (Marty Daly, John Sandberg, and Jim Wood), Roberto Brandeo, Karen Brennan, Jessica Brod Millner, Bart Bronk, Anne Brooks, Kathleen Burke, Jessica Cabeen, John Checkley, Po Chung, Amy Coon, Alan Cooper, Ruth Cross, Arthur Culbert, Claudia Daggett, Brittney Dailey, Claudia Davis, Moshe Dear, Christine Desrochers, Tricia Diebold, Carla Duncan, Paul Fanuele, Rachelle Finck, Kathleen Fink, Adrianne Finley Odell, Patrick Fisher, Michael Flynn, Barbara Gallant, Howard Gardner, Bahram Ghaseminejad, Vivian Gibson, Molly Gleason, Janine Gorrell, Karen Guskin, Natassia Hamer, Mark Harrington, Terry Harris, Chris Hass, Sophia Hayes, Betsey Heeney, Craig Hinkle, Mimi Hirshberg, Jen Holshouser, Bill Hudson, Cathy Hulet, Joel Hunter, Joy Hurd, Dana Januszka, Misty Johnson, Steve Kaio-Maddox, Kelly Kaiser, Kevin Kerwin, Beth Kisiel, Jennifer Koener, Lisa Koplik, Mindy Kornhaber, Krista Leh, Jane Levy, Erin Lozouwski, Lisa Maher, Carolyn Manard, Kim Marshall, Masa Massenburg-Johnson, Mrs. Helen Mayfield (my 1st grade teacher), the staff at the Meshuggah Café on Delmar Boulevard, Lynn Monaco, Jami Mundt, Tamera Musiowsky-Borneman, Alison Nash, Kim Nugent, Hannah Owens, Emmie Pawlak, Roger Perry, Devin Quinlan, Johanna Ricker, Jennifer Roberts, Juan Roncal, Michelle Rooks, Michel Saw, Caryn Sawlis, Dan Schwartz, Erin Schulte, Keith Shahan, Katie Small, Alison Smith, Maureen Smith, Ed Soule, Susan Stawas, Libby Stogdill, Lori Stollar, Laura Sweat, Stephanie Teachout, Barbara Thomson, Dennis Toliver, Chris Truffer, Laura Varlas, Chris Wallach, Connie White, Jane Williams, Kimberley Williams, and Leslie Windler.

Deep gratitude goes to the staff members at the New City School in St. Louis, Missouri, a diverse and innovative institution that I led for 34 years. I was very fortunate to work with so many incredibly talented educators, kind and caring families, and supportive Boards of Trustees. New City was a school of learners of all ages, so I eagerly went to work every day (OK, most days). Our faculty began implementing the theory of multiple intelligences in 1988, and my appreciation for the intrapersonal and interpersonal intelligences kindled my desire to learn more about SEL (and this was years before the Kindle!). A previous book of mine, *The Art of School Leadership*, captured the lessons I learned while working at New City School, and some appear in these pages as well.

I retired from New City in 2015, and now, in my life's next chapter, I am teaching in the Educational Leadership and Policy Studies program at the University of Missouri–St. Louis. I enjoy working and learning with my graduate students and colleagues. Thanks to the previous dean, Carole Basile (now dean of the Teachers College at Arizona State University), for pulling me into the higher education fold, and special appreciation goes to Dean Ann Taylor for her leadership and support. It's really a treat to teach.

The staff at ASCD has always been helpful to me. However good and crisp my writing may be, the bulk of the credit for this goes to Naomi Thiers and Teresa Preston at *Educational Leadership*, the skilled folks who edited my "Principal Connection" column for 14 years. They taught me a lot as they routinely turned my farrago of words into smooth and readable sentences. Thanks to them and to editors Marge Scherer and Anthony Rebora for support and confidence that they gave to my column. Likewise, whenever I meet with Genny Ostertag, ASCD's Director of Content Acquisitions, I know that she will be a fount of enthusiasm and good ideas. She and I go way back (despite her youth!) and her ideas have helped me conceptualize and refine several books. Editors are golden (good ones, anyway), and I have lucked out by getting to work twice with Liz Wegner. She was extraordinarily helpful with my last book, *The Formative Five: Fostering Grit, Empathy, and Other Success Skills Every Student Needs*, and I was delighted to be able to work with her on this volume. She brings incredible skills and patience, and I need both.

Almost last and far from least, special applause goes to Karleen, my wife, for her confidence, flexibility, and patience (there's that word again), and to C.J. and Callie, our two standard poodles who don't know they're dogs. To be fair, we sometimes forget that, too! They are great company and never feel a need to edit my writing.

Last, thanks to you, dear reader. The fact that you are reading a book that focuses on students' SEL means that you are an educator that our students need. The only thing we can safely predict about the future is that it will change in ways we cannot foresee, so we must prepare our students by helping them become good and caring people who will play a positive role in communities, organizations, and families. I hope that this book is a helpful tool for you.

We're all in this together, so I would be delighted to hear what works, what doesn't, and what questions you may have. You can visit my website—www.thomasrhoerr.com—or contact me at trhoerr@aol.com or trhoerr@newcityschool.org.

References

American Heart Association. (2018, May 15). Limit screen time and get your kids (and the whole family) moving. Retrieved from https://www.heart.org/en /healthy-living/fitness/getting-active/limit-screen-time-and-get-your-kids-and -the-whole-family-moving

Anda, R. (n.d.). *The adverse childhood experiences study: Child abuse and public health.* Chicago: Prevent Child Abuse America. Retrieved from http://www .preventchildabuse.org/images/docs/anda_wht_ppr.pdf

Anderson, M. (2016). *Learning to choose, choosing to learn: The key to student motivation and achievement.* Alexandria, VA: ASCD.

Angelou, M. (1969). *I know why the caged bird sings.* New York: Random House.

Aspen Institute. (2019). *From a nation at risk to a nation at hope: Recommendations from the National Commission on Social, Emotional, and Academic Development.* Executive summary. Retrieved from http://nationathope.org/wp-content/ uploads/aspen_final-report_execsumm_final_forweb.pdf

Ayshford, E. (2018, April 2). How a room's lighting shapes our decisions. *Kellogg Insight.* Retrieved from https://insight.kellogg.northwestern.edu/article/ how-lighting-affects-choices

Baron-Cohen, S. (2011). *Zero degrees of empathy: A new theory of human cruelty.* New York: Penguin Group.

Barshay, J. (2019, March 11). Research scholars to air problems with using 'grit' at school. *The Hechinger Report.* Retrieved from https://hechingerreport.org/ research-scholars-to-air-problems-with-using-grit-at-school/

Barth, R. S. (1990). *Improving schools from within: Teachers, parents, and principals can make the difference.* San Francisco: Jossey-Bass.

Beals, M. (1994). *Warriors don't cry: A searing memoir of the battle to integrate Little Rock's Central High.* New York: Pocket Books.

Berdan, B. (2016, October 6). Participation trophies send a dangerous message. *New York Times.* Retrieved from https://www.nytimes.com/roomfordebate/2016/10/06/should-every-young-athlete-get-a-trophy/participation-trophies-send-a-dangerous-message

Berkowitz, M. W., Bier, M. C., & McCauley, B. (2016, July). *Effective features and practices that support character development.* Paper presented at the National Academies of Sciences, Engineering, and Medicine Workshop on Defining and Measuring Character and Character Education, Washington, DC.

Berman, S., Chaffee, S., & Sarmiento, J. (2018). The practice base for how we learn: Supporting students' social, emotional, and academic development. *The Aspen Institute.* Retrieved from https://www.aspeninstitute.org/publications/practice-base-learn-supporting-students-social-emotional-academic-development/

Blad, E. (2018, March 9). Spreading social-emotional learning across all schools. *Education Week, 37*(24), 8. Retrieved from https://www.edweek.org/ew/articles/2018/03/09/how-one-district-is-spreading-social-emotional-learning.html

Blight, D. (2018). *Frederick Douglass: Prophet of freedom.* New York: Simon & Schuster.

Bloom, P. (2016). *Against empathy: The case for rational compassion.* New York: HarperCollins.

Borba, M. (2016). *Unselfie: Why empathetic kids succeed in our all-about-me world.* New York: Touchstone.

Boyles, N. (2018, October). Learning character from characters. *Educational Leadership, 76*(2), 70–74. Retrieved from http://www.ascd.org/publications/educational-leadership/oct18/vol76/num02/Learning-Character-from-Characters.aspx

Brandao, R. (2018, November 27). 4 ways to teach empathy in the classroom. *Education Dive.* Retrieved from https://www.educationdive.com/news/4-ways-to-teach-empathy-in-the-classroom/542323/

Brooks, D. (2019). *The second mountain: The quest for a moral life.* New York: Random House.

Brotto, G. (2018, June 4). The future of education depends on social emotional learning: Here's why. *EdSurge.* Retrieved from https://www.edsurge.com/news/2018-06-04-the-future-of-education-depends-on-social-emotional-learning-here-s-why

Brown, B. (2010, June). The power of vulnerability. *TED Talk.* Retrieved from https://www.ted.com/talks/brene_brown_on_vulnerability?language=en

Brown, B. (2015). *Rising strong: How the ability to reset transforms the way we live, love, parent, and lead.* New York: Penguin Random House.

Brown, B. (2018). *Dare to lead: Brave work, tough conversations, whole hearts.* New York: Penguin Random House.

Bruni, F. (2015). *Where you go is not who you'll be: An antidote to the college admissions mania.* New York: Hachette Group.

Bryant, A. (2017, April 21). Corner office: Leila Janah on knowing when to let go. *New York Times.* Retrieved from https://www.nytimes.com/2017/04/21/business/leila-janah-samasource-lxmi.html

Cain, S. (2012). *Quiet: The power of introverts in a world that can't stop talking*. New York: Random House.

Calarco, J. M. (2018, June 1). Why rich kids are so good at the marshmallow test. *The Atlantic*. Retrieved from https://www.theatlantic.com/family/archive/2018/06/marshmallow-test/561779/

Charyn, J. (2019). *The perilous adventures of the Cowboy King: A novel of Teddy Roosevelt and his times*. New York: Liveright Publishing Company.

Cho, J. H. (2016, May 25). "Diversity is being invited to the party; inclusion is being asked to dance," Verna Myers tells Cleveland Bar. *The Plain Dealer*. Retrieved from https://articles.cleveland.com/business/index.ssf/2016/05/diversity_is_being_invited_to.amp

Chung, P., with Elfassy, R. (2016). *The 12 dimensions of a service leader*. New York: Lexingford Publishing.

Cloud, H. (2009). *Integrity: The courage to meet the demands of reality*. New York: HarperBusiness.

Coates, T. (2015). *Between the world and me*. New York: Spiegel & Grau.

Coleman, J. (2013, May 6). Six components of a great corporate culture. *Harvard Business Review*. Retrieved from https://hbr.org/2013/05/six-components-of-culture

Common Sense Media. (2015, November 3). *The Common Sense census: Media use by tweens and teens*. San Francisco: Author. Retrieved from https://www.commonsensemedia.org/sites/default/files/uploads/research/census_researchreport.pdf

Cowen, T. (2017). *The complacent class: The self-defeating quest for the American Dream*. New York: St. Martin's Press.

Coyle, D. (2018). *The culture code: The secret of highly successful groups*. New York: Bantam Books.

Daniels, M. (2018, November 28). For college admissions, let's value grit over GPA. *Washington Post*. Retrieved from https://www.washingtonpost.com/opinions/for-college-admissions-lets-value-grit-over-gpas/2018/11/28/8aa1c9c4-ed09-11e8-8679-934a2b33be52_story.html?utm_term=.2064eb7a5a43

Davidson, C. (2012). *Now you see it: How technology and brain science will transform schools and businesses for the 21st century*. New York: Penguin Books.

de Waal, F. (2019) *Mama's last hug: Animal emotions and what they tell us about ourselves*. New York: W. W. Norton & Company.

DeWitt, P. (2018, April 2). 7 simple steps to create a positive school climate. *Education Week*. Retrieved from https://blogs.edweek.org/edweek/finding_common_ground/2018/04/7_simple_steps_to_create_a_positive_school_climate.html

Doorley, S., & Witthoft, S. (2012). *Make space: How to set the stage for creative collaboration*. Hoboken, NJ: John Wiley & Sons.

Duhigg, C. (2012). *The power of habit: Why we do what we do in life and business*. New York: Random House.

Duhigg, C. (2016, February 25). What Google learned from its quest to build the perfect team. *New York Times Magazine*. Retrieved from https://www.nytimes.com/2016/02/28/magazine/what-google-learned-from-its-quest-to-build-the-perfect-team.html

Durlak, J. A., Weissberg, R. P., Dymnicki, A. B., Taylor, R. D., & Schellinger, K. B. (2011). The impact of enhancing students' social and emotional learning: A meta-analysis of school-based universal interventions. *Child Development, 82*(1): 405–432.

Dweck, C. (2007). *Mindset: The new psychology of success.* New York: Penguin.

Elliott, Z., & Wong, P. (2016). *Milo's museum.* CreateSpace.

Elmore, T. (2011). *Habitudes: The art of leading others.* Norcross, GA: Growing Leaders.

Evans, R. (2010). *Seven secrets of a savvy school leader: A guide to surviving and thriving.* San Francisco: Jossey-Bass.

Fensterwald, J. (2019, June 5). There's value but also limitations to students' grading their own interpersonal skills, study finds. *EdSource.* Retrieved from https://edsource.org/2019/theres-value-but-also-limitations-to-students-grading-their-own-interpersonal-skills-study-finds/613326

Fingerhut, H. (2018, June 14). Most Americans express positive views of the country's growing racial and ethnic diversity. *FactTank.* Pew Research Center. Retrieved from https://www.pewresearch.org/fact-tank/2018/06/14/most-americans-express-positive-views-of-countrys-growing-racial-and-ethnic-diversity/

Finn, C. E. (2017, June 21). The dirt-encrusted roots of social-emotional learning. *Education Week, 36*(36), 2.

Folkman, J. (2018, November 25). What great problem solvers do differently. *Forbes.* Retrieved from https://www.forbes.com/sites/joefolkman/2018/11/25/what-great-problem-solvers-do-differently/#7551d0222566

Freiberg, K., & Freiberg, J. (2019, January 4). 20 reasons why Herb Kelleher was one of the most beloved leaders of our time. *Forbes.* Retrieved from https://www.forbes.com/sites/kevinandjackiefreiberg/2019/01/04/20-reasons-why-herb-kelleher-was-one-of-the-most-beloved-leaders-of-our-time/#78e99dc6b311

Frey, W. H. (2018, March 14). The US will become "minority white" in 2045, Census projects: Youthful minorities are the engine of future growth [blog post]. *The Avenue.* Retrieved from https://www.brookings.edu/blog/the-avenue/2018/03/14/the-us-will-become-minority-white-in-2045-census-projects/

Friedman, T. (2016). *Thank you for being late: An optimist's guide to thriving in the age of accelerations.* New York: Picador.

Fullan, M. (2014). *The principal: Three keys to maximizing impact.* New York: John Wiley.

Gardner, H. (1983). *Frames of mind: The theory of multiple intelligences.* New York: Basic Books.

Gardner, H. (2006). *Five minds for the future.* Cambridge, MA: Harvard Business School Press.

Gawande, A. (2011, October 3). Personal best: Top athletes and singers have coaches. Should you? *New Yorker.* Retrieved from https://www.newyorker.com/magazine/2011/10/03/personal-best

Goleman, D. (1995). *Emotional intelligence: Why it can matter more than IQ.* New York: Bantam Press.

Goleman, D. (2007, June 12). Three kinds of empathy: Cognitive, emotional, compassionate. Retrieved from http://www.danielgoleman.info/three-kinds-of-empathy-cognitive-emotional-compassionate/

Goold, D. (2019, January 21). Shildt "shoots straight" with Cardinals, emphasizes trust and communication. *St. Louis Post-Dispatch*. Retrieved from https://www.stltoday.com/sports/baseball/professional/shildt-shoots-straight-with-cardinals-emphasizes-trust-and-communication/article_7b9dc1b0-dbf4-58b9-aeb7-92d86d2616d3.html

Gresham, F. M. (2018). *Effective interventions for social-emotional learning*. New York: Guilford Press.

Groysberg, B., Lee, J., Price, J., & Cheng, J. (2018, January-February). The leader's guide to corporate culture. *Harvard Business Review*. Retrieved from https://hbr.org/product/the-leaders-guide-to-corporate-culture/R1801B-PDF-ENG

Harari, Y. (2017). *Homo deus: A brief history of tomorrow*. New York: HarperCollins.

Heckman, J. J. (2013). *Give kids a fair chance*. Cambridge, MA: MIT Press.

Heffernan, M. (2015). Forget the pecking order at work. *TED Women*. Retrieved from https://www.ted.com/talks/margaret_heffernan_why_it_s_time_to_forget_the_pecking_order_at_work?language=en

Heick, T. (2018, December 23). The problem with most school mission statements. *TeachThought*. Retrieved from https://www.teachthought.com/education/school-mission-statement-hogwash/

Heimans, J., & Timms, H. (2018). *New power: How power works in our hyperconnected world—and how to make it work for you*. New York: Doubleday.

Hickman, H. H., Jr. (1998). *Rocket boys*. New York: Random House.

Hoerr, T. R. (2008/2009, December/January). Data that count. *Educational Leadership, 66*(4), 93–94. Retrieved from http://www.ascd.org/publications/educational-leadership/dec08/vol66/num04/Data-That-Count.aspx

Hoerr, T. R. (2009a, April). The rule of six. *Educational Leadership. 66*(7), 83–84. Retrieved from http://www.ascd.org/publications/educational-leadership/apr09/vol66/num07/The-Rule-of-Six.aspx

Hoerr, T. R. (2009b, December 1). What if faculty meetings were voluntary? *Education Week, 29*(13), 26–27. Retrieved from http://www.edweek.org/ew/articles/2009/12/02/13hoerr.h29.html

Hoerr, T. R. (2012, March). Got grit? *Educational Leadership, 69*(6), 84–85. Retrieved from http://www.ascd.org/publications/educational-leadership/mar12/vol69/num06/Got-Grit%C2%A2.aspx

Hoerr, T. R. (2013). *Fostering grit: How do I prepare my students for the real world?* Alexandria, VA: ASCD.

Hoerr, T. R. (2015, March). Responding to Ferguson. *Educational Leadership 72*(6), 85–86. Retrieved from http://www.ascd.org/publications/educational-leadership/mar15/vol72/num06/Responding-to-Ferguson.aspx

Hoerr, T. R. (2015/2016, December/January). What does your restroom say about your school? *Educational Leadership, 73*(4), 88–89. Retrieved from http://www.ascd.org/publications/educational-leadership/dec15/vol73/num04/What-Does-Your-Restroom-Say-About-Your-School%C2%A2.aspx

Hoerr, T. R. (2016, April). Why you need a diversity champion. *Educational Leadership, 73*(7), 86–87. Retrieved from http://www.ascd.org/publications/educational-leadership/apr16/vol73/num07/Why-You-Need-a-Diversity-Champion.aspx

Hoerr, T. R. (2017). *The formative five: Fostering grit, empathy, and other success skills every student needs.* Alexandria, VA: ASCD.

Hoerr, T. R. (2018a, April). Building empathy in schools. *Educational Leadership, 75*(7), 86–87. Retrieved from http://www.ascd.org/publications/educational-leadership/apr18/vol75/num07/Building-Empathy-in-Schools.aspx

Hoerr, T. R. (2018b, December 11). The five success skills every student should master. *EdWeek.* Retrieved from https://www.edweek.org/ew/articles/2018/12/12/the-five-success-skills-every-student-should.html

Holmes, A. (2015, October 27). Has diversity lost its meaning? *New York Times.* Retrieved from https://www.nytimes.com/2015/11/01/magazine/has-diversity-lost-its-meaning.html

Isaacson, W. (2012, April). The real leadership lessons of Steve Jobs. *Harvard Business Review.* Retrieved from https://hbr.org/2012/04/the-real-leadership-lessons-of-steve-jobs

Isaacson, W. (2014, October 7). Why Steve Jobs obsessed about office design (and, yes, bathroom locations). *LinkedIn.* Retrieved from https://www.linkedin.com/pulse/20141007161621-73685339-why-steve-jobs-obsessed-about-office-design-and-yes-bathroom-locations/

Ito, J., & Howe, J. (2016). *Whiplash: How to survive our faster future.* New York: Hachette Book Group.

Jackson, J. L., Sr. (2018, December 30). New Year's Day is also Emancipation Day. *New York Times.* Retrieved from https://www.nytimes.com/2018/12/30/opinion/new-years-day-emancipation-proclamation.html

Jacobs, H. H. (2014). *Leading the new literacies.* Bloomington, IN: Solution Tree.

Kahn, A., & Bouie, J. (2015, June 25). The Atlantic slave trade in two minutes. *Slate.* Retrieved from http://www.slate.com/articles/life/the_history_of_american_slavery/2015/06/animated_interactive_of_the_history_of_the_atlantic_slave_trade.html

Kahneman, D. (2011). *Thinking, fast and slow.* New York: Farrar, Strauss and Giroux.

Killinger, B. (2010). *Integrity: Doing the right thing for the right reason.* Montreal, Quebec, Canada: McGill-Queen's University Press.

Koch, C. (1996, March 15). The bright stuff. *CIO Magazine.* Retrieved from http://psych.utoronto.ca/users/reingold/courses/intelligence/cache/031596_qa-content.html

Koehn. N. (2017). *Forged in crisis: The power of courageous leadership in turbulent times.* New York: Scribner.

Kurtzman. J. (1999, January 1). An interview with Howard Gardner. *Strategy + Business.* Retrieved from https://www.strategy-business.com/article/10279?gko=c1897

Lepore, J. (2018). *These truths: A history of the United States.* New York: W. W. Norton & Company.

Levenson, E., & Morales, M. (2019, March 13). Wealthy parents, actresses, coaches, among those charged in massive college cheating admission scandal, federal prosecutors say. *CNN.* Retrieved from https://www.cnn.com/2019/03/12/us/college-admission-cheating-scheme/index.html

Lickona, T., & Davidson, M. (2005). *Smart and good high schools: Integrating excellence and ethics for success in school, work, and beyond.* Cortland, NY: Center for the 4th and 5th Rs (Respect and Responsibility).

Lindsey, R., Robins, K., & Terrell, R. (2009). *Cultural proficiency: A manual for school leaders.* Thousand Oaks, CA: Sage Publications.

Love, B. L. (2019, February 12). 'Grit is in our DNA': Why teaching grit is inherently anti-black. *Education Week.* Retrieved from https://www.edweek.org/ew/articles/2019/02/13/grit-is-in-our-dna-why-teaching.html

Lumpkin, L. (2018, December 16). Diversity and inclusion course could become graduation requirement for Anne Arundel students. *The Capital Gazette.* Retrieved from https://www.capitalgazette.com/news/schools/ac-cn-global-citizenship-20181215-story.html

Madhani, A. (2018, May 23). Poll: Approval of same-sex marriage in U.S. reaches new high. *USA Today.* Retrieved from https://www.usatoday.com/story/news/nation/2018/05/23/same-sex-marriage-poll-americans/638587002/

Mahoney, J. L., Durlak, J. A., & Weissberg, R. (2018, November 26). An update on social and emotional learning outcome research. *Kappan Newsletter.* Retrieved from https://www.kappanonline.org/social-emotional-learning-outcome-research-mahoney-durlak-weissberg/

Mahoney, J. L., & Weissberg, R. P. (2018, October). SEL: What the research says. *Educational Leadership, 76*(2), 34–35. Retrieved from http://www.ascd.org/publications/educational-leadership/oct18/vol76/num02/SEL@-What-the-Research-Says.aspx

Massachusetts General Hospital. (2019, January 14). Virtual video visits may improve patient convenience without sacrificing quality of care, communication. *MGH Press Release.* Retrieved from https://www.massgeneral.org/News/pressrelease.aspx?id=2338

McKibben, S. (2018, October). Grit and the greater good: A conversation with Angela Duckworth. *Educational Leadership, 76*(2), 40–45. Retrieved from http://www.ascd.org/publications/educational-leadership/oct18/vol76/num02/Grit-and-the-Greater-Good@-A-Conversation-with-Angela-Duckworth.aspx

Meacham, J. (2018). *The soul of America: The battle for our better angels.* New York: Random House.

Menzel, M., & Mann, C. (1995). *Material world: A global family portrait.* Berkeley, CA: Ten Speed Press.

Mischel, W. (2014). *The marshmallow test: Mastering self-control.* New York: Little, Brown and Company.

Moore, E., Michael, A., & Penick-Parks, M. (Eds.). (2018). *The guide for white women who teach black boys.* Thousand Oaks, CA: Corwin.

Moore, W. (2011). *The other Wes Moore: One name, two fates.* New York: Spiegel & Grau.

Morgan, K. (2019, February 25). A guide to changing someone else's beliefs: Use the science of persuasion to your advantage. *Medium.* Retrieved from https://medium.com/s/reasonable-doubt/a-guide-to-changing-someone-elses-beliefs-c08fc1cb956b

Morin A. (2017, August 22). We're raising a generation of wimpy kids . . . and the kids are paying the price. *Psychology Today.* Retrieved from https://www.psychologytoday.com/us/blog/what-mentally-strong-people-dont-do/201708/were-raising-generation-wimpy-kids

Muller, J. Z. (2018). *The tyranny of metrics.* Princeton, New Jersey: Princeton University Press.

National Commission on Excellence in Education. (1983). *A nation at risk: The imperative for educational reform.* Washington, DC: Author.

NPR. (2018, September 11). The power of expectations [Video file]. Retrieved from https://www.youtube.com/watch?v=hbhwlRRW_3o

Obama, M. (2018). *Becoming.* New York: Crown.

Pink, D. (2009). *Drive: The surprising truth about what motivates us.* New York: Penguin.

Posey, A. (2018, June 14). How to support the emotional link to learning. *ASCD Express, 13*(19). Retrieved from http://www.ascd.org/ascd-express/vol13/1319-posey.aspx

Premack, R. (2018, July 12). One of the biggest problems facing self-driving trucks has little to do with the technology. *Business Insider.* Retrieved from https://www.businessinsider.com/autonomous-trucks-self-driving-trucks-laws-2018-7

Robert Wood Johnson Foundation. (n.d.). *Social and emotional learning.* Retrieved from https://www.rwjf.org/en/library/collections/social-and-emotional-learning.html

Robert Wood Johnson Foundation. (2018, December 1). Social and emotional development matters: Taking action now for future generations. Retrieved from https://www.rwjf.org/en/library/research/2018/12/social-and-emotional-development-matters.html Robinson, K. (2006). Do schools kill creativity? *TED Talk.* Retrieved from https://www.ted.com/talks/ken_robinson_says_schools_kill_creativity?language=en

Satariano, A., Peltier, E., & Kostyukov, D. (2018, November 27). Meet Zora, The robot caregiver. *New York Times.* Retrieved from https://www.nytimes.com/interactive/2018/11/23/technology/robot-nurse-zora.html

Satell, G. (2018, October 13). These are the skills that your kids will need for the future (hint: it's not coding). *Inc.* Retrieved from https://www.inc.com/greg-satell/here-are-skills-that-your-kids-will-need-for-future-hint-its-not-coding.html

Schonert-Reichl, K. (2017, Spring). Social and emotional learning and teachers. *The Future of Children.* NJ: Princeton-Brookings. 27(1). Retrieved from https://www.wallacefoundation.org/knowledge-center/Documents/FOC-Spring-Vol27-No1-Compiled-Future-of-Children-spring-2017.pdf

Schwab, K. (2019, January 23). Doctor's offices are terrifying: This one is designed to calm your nerves. *Fast Company.* Retrieved from https://www.fastcompany.com/90295058/doctors-offices-are-terrifying-this-one-is-designed-to-calm-your-nerves

Smith, A. (2002). *The no. 1 ladies' detective agency*. New York: Anchor Books.

Starr, J. (2019, March 21). Can we keep SEL on course? *Kappan Online*. Retrieved from https://www.kappanonline.org/can-we-keep-sel-on-course-social-emotional-learning-starr/

Sultan, A. (2018, November 23). A better way to teach empathy. *St. Louis Post-Dispatch*. Retrieved from https://www.stltoday.com/lifestyles/parenting/aisha-sultan/sultan-a-better-way-to-teach-empathy/article_5663e332-9dd1-5d9d-ab69-b385157de4be.html

Szalavitz, M. (2010, May). Shocker: Empathy levels dropped 40% in college students since 2000. *Psychology Today*. Retrieved from https://www.psychologytoday.com/us/blog/born-love/201005shocker-empathy-dropped-40-in-college-students-2000

Tavernise, S. (2018, September 13). U.S. has highest share of foreign born since 1910, with more coming from Asia. *New York Times*. Retrieved from https://www.nytimes.com/2018/09/13/us/census-foreign-population.html

Tedesco, J. (2017). Effecting change at scale: The concentric circle approach. *LinkedIn*. Retrieved from https://www.linkedin.com/pulse/effecting-change-scale-concentric-circle-approach-john-tedesco

Tochluk, S. (2010). *Witnessing whiteness: The need to talk about race and how to do it*. Lanham, MD: Rowman and Littlefield.

Torres, C. (2019, February). Assessment as an act of love. *Education Update, 61*(2), 2. Retrieved from http://www.ascd.org/publications/newsletters/education-up-date/feb19/vol61/num02/Assessment-as-an-Act-of-Love.aspx

Tough, P. (2011, November 18). What if the secret to success is failure? *New York Times Magazine*. Retrieved from http://www.nytimes.com/2011/09/18/maga-zine/what-if-the-secret-to-success-is-failure.html

Tough, P. (2012). *How children succeed: Grit, curiosity, and the hidden power of charac-ter*. New York: Random House.

Tough, P. (2016, June). How kids learn resilience. *The Atlantic*. Retrieved from https://www.theatlantic.com/magazine/archive/2016/06/how-kids-really-succeed/480744/

Trout, J. D. (2009). *The empathy gap: Building bridges to the good life and the good soci-ety*. New York: Penguin.

Van Teeseling, I. (2019, January 2) How are we going to teach our kids to be bal-anced people if we aren't? *The Big Smoke*. Retrieved from https://thebigsmoke.com/2019/01/02/how-are-we-going-to-teach-our-kids-to-be-balanced-people-if-we-arent/

Ward, J. (2017). *Sing, unburied, sing*. New York: Simon & Schuster.

Warren, R. P. (1946). *All the King's men*. Boston: Houghton Mifflin Harcourt.

Watkins, M. D. (2013, May 15). What is organizational culture? And why should we care? *Harvard Business Review*. Retrieved from https://hbr.org/2013/05/what-is-organizational-culture

Weick, K. (1996a, May/June). Prepare your organization to fight fires. *Harvard Business, 74*(3). Retrieved from https://hbr.org/1996/05/prepare-your-organization-to-fight-fires

Weick, K. E. (1996b, June). Drop your tools: An allegory for organizational studies. *Administrative Science Quarterly, 41*(2), 301–313.

Welch, A. (2018, August 6). Health experts say parents need to drastically cut kids' screen time. *CBS News.* Retrieved from https://www.cbsnews.com/news/parents-need-to-drastically-cut-kids-screen-time-devices-american-heart-association/

Westover, T. (2018). *Educated: A memoir.* New York: Random House.

Williams, J. (2018, April 20). Segregation's legacy. *U.S. News & World Report.* Retrieved from https://www.usnews.com/news/the-report/articles/2018-04-20/us-is-still-segregated-even-after-fair-housing-act

Wise, T. (2004). *White like me: Reflections on race from a privileged son.* Berkley, CA. Soft Skull Press.

Zimbardo, P (2008). The psychology of evil. *TED Talk.* Retrieved from https://www.ted.com/talks/philip_zimbardo_on_the_psychology_of_evil/transcript?language=en

Zimmer, C. (2018). *She has her mother's laugh: The powers, perversions, and potential of heredity.* New York: Penguin Random House.

Index

The letter *f* following a page number denotes a figure.

189

About the Author

 **Thomas R. Hoerr** retired after leading the New City School in St. Louis, Missouri, for 34 years and is now the Emeritus Head of School. He teaches in the educational leadership program at the University of Missouri–St. Louis and holds a PhD from Washington University in St. Louis. Hoerr has written five books—*Becoming a Multiple Intelligences School* (2000), *The Art of School Leadership* (2005), *School Leadership for the Future* (2009), *Fostering Grit* (2013), and *The Formative Five: Fostering Grit, Empathy, and Other Success Skills Every Student Needs* (2017)—and more than 150 articles, including "The Principal Connection" column in *Educational Leadership*. Hoerr is a fan of chocolate and an enthusiastic but poor basketball player. Readers who would like to continue the dialogue may contact him at trhoerr@newcityschool.org or trhoerr@aol.com.

Related ASCD Resources

At the time of publication, the following resources were available (ASCD stock numbers in parentheses).

Print Products

All Learning Is Social and Emotional: Helping Students Develop Essential Skills for the Classroom and Beyond by Nancy Frey, Douglas Fisher, and Dominique Smith (#119033)

The Formative Five: Fostering Grit, Empathy, and Other Success Skills Every Student Needs by Thomas R. Hoerr (#116043)

Fostering Grit: How do I prepare my students for the real world? (ASCD Arias) by Thomas R. Hoerr (#SF113075)

Fostering Resilient Learners: Strategies for Creating a Trauma-Sensitive Classroom by Kristin Souers with Pete Hall (#116014)

Nurturing Habits of Mind in Early Childhood: Success Stories from Classrooms Around the World edited by Arthur L. Costa and Bena O. Kallick (#119017)

Relationship, Responsibility, and Regulation: Trauma-Invested Practices for Fostering Resilient Learners by Kristin Van Marter Souers with Pete Hall (#119027)

For up-to-date information about ASCD resources, go to www.ascd.org. You can search the complete archives of Educational Leadership at www.ascd.org/el.

ASCD myTeachSource®
Download resources from a professional learning platform with hundreds of research-based best practices and tools for your classroom at http://myteachsource.ascd.org/

For more information, send an e-mail to member@ascd.org; call 1-800-933-2723 or 703-578-9600; send a fax to 703-575-5400; or write to Information Services, ASCD, 1703 N. Beauregard St., Alexandria, VA 22311-1714 USA.

WHOLE CHILD
TENETS

The ASCD Whole Child approach is an effort to transition from a focus on narrowly defined academic achievement to one that promotes the long-term development and success of all children. Through this approach, ASCD supports educators, families, community members, and policymakers as they move from a vision about educating the whole child to sustainable, collaborative actions.

Taking Social-Emotional Learning Schoolwide relates to **all five** tenets.

For more about the ASCD Whole Child approach, visit ***www.ascd.org/wholechild.***

1 HEALTHY
Each student enters school healthy and learns about and practices a healthy lifestyle.

2 SAFE
Each student learns in an environment that is physically and emotionally safe for students and adults.

3 ENGAGED
Each student is actively engaged in learning and is connected to the school and broader community.

4 SUPPORTED
Each student has access to personalized learning and is supported by qualified, caring adults.

5 CHALLENGED
Each student is challenged academically and prepared for success in college or further study and for employment and participation in a global environment.